W9-AAE-877

NOTES ON BRAHMS

NOTES ON BRAHMS

20 Crucial Works

Conrad Wilson

William B. Eerdmans Publishing Company
Grand Rapids, Michigan

For Sue, who put up with my late hours and the clutter of books and CDs while this and the other books were being written.

© 2005 Conrad Wilson
All rights reserved

First published 2005 by
SAINT ANDREW PRESS
Edinburgh

This edition published 2005
in the United States of America by
Wm. B. Eerdmans Publishing Company
255 Jefferson Ave. S.E., Grand Rapids, Michigan 49503

Printed in the United States of America

10 09 08 07 06 05   7 6 5 4 3 2 1

ISBN-10: 0-8028-2991-0
ISBN-13: 978-0-8028-2991-7

www.eerdmans.com

CONTENTS

NOTES ON BRAHMS

FOREWORD

Why twenty? Obviously it is a device, one way of drawing attention to some of the masterpieces in a great composer's output. But at the same time it is a discipline and a challenge. Why choose these particular works and not others? The question and its answers are my reason for writing this book and its companions on other composers. In making my selection, I thought twenty works to be a good, sufficiently tight number. Increase it to thirty and choice becomes easier, perhaps too easy. Reduce it to ten and, in the case of great productive composers, you don't really have enough music wholly to justify what you are doing. Too many crucial works would have to be excluded, and the gaps would be glaring. So twenty it is, though not in the sense of a top twenty, because a crucial work does not actually have to be a great one, and the works are not listed – how could they be? – in any order of merit.

But each of them, it seems to me, needs to mark a special moment in its composer's life – perhaps a turning point, perhaps a sudden flash of inspiration, perhaps an intensifying of genius, as when Schubert produced his setting of Goethe's 'Gretchen am Spinnrade' at the age of 17, or Mozart his G major Violin Concerto, K216, at 19, or Brahms his First Piano Concerto at 25.

Yet none of these composers was a prodigy as gifted as Mendelssohn, whose String Octet and whose *A Midsummer Night's Dream* overture were the most astounding teenage masterpieces of all time. But if there was nothing so arresting to be found among Mozart's or Schubert's numerous boyhood works, and certainly nothing among Brahms's, the change when it came was startling.

With Schubert's first great song, Mozart's first great concerto, Beethoven's and Mendelssohn's first great pieces of chamber music and Brahms's lengthy but inexorable perfecting of his First Piano Concerto came the shock of surprise in the form of an audacious new command of melody and accompaniment, a conspicuous leap in quality and, in the slow movement of the Mozart, a grasp of the mystery of beauty which made his two previous violin concertos, written in the same year, seem blandly impersonal exercises in composition.

Yet this third of Mozart's five violin concertos is not a masterpiece in the sense that *Don Giovanni* is, just as Schubert's boyhood String Quartet in E flat major, D87, for all its melodic beauty, is not as overwhelming as 'Death and the Maiden'. Nor, for that matter, does the fizz of Mendelssohn's early string symphonies have the passion of his A minor String Quartet, written very soon afterwards. Brahms's First Piano Concerto, on the other hand, is surely as great a work as he ever wrote.

It is not the aim of these books to set one masterpiece against another, or to suggest that early works are automatically less interesting than late ones. To regard a composer's output purely as a process of evolution is to fail inexcusably to accept a work on its own terms – a serious flaw in assessments of Schubert, who, according to many a pundit, did not 'find' himself until he was almost dead. In Mendelssohn, the division between what is 'early' and what is 'late' and what is the difference between them becomes less and less clearly demarcated.

So, early works are not being banned from these pages, even if it means the loss of some late ones. Nor is my decision to deal with the music chronologically based on any intrinsic belief that it reflects in some special way a composer's progress. The intention is simply to shed light on what was happening to him at the time he wrote a particular piece, where he was, what he was doing or experiencing, and how the music fits into the general pattern of his life and output. To go beyond this, by claiming that Haydn, for example, 'progressed' from his *Storm and Stress* symphonies to his *London* ones, or Mozart from his E flat major Piano Concerto, K271, to his E flat major, K482, is to undervalue his achievement as a whole.

So, no masterpiece has been omitted simply because its composer later in some way surpassed it. Some works are included simply because I adore them, or am prepared to defend them against the judgement of people who detest them. Liking a piece of music, we should always remember, is not the opposite of disliking it. It is a different condition altogether, and being able to explain why we like it is perhaps more important in the end than pronouncing on whether it is good music or bad.

Each of these twenty short essays is a species of what are traditionally known as programme notes – the descriptions to be found in printed concert or opera programmes of what is being performed that night. Donald Francis Tovey, one-time professor of music at Edinburgh University, was a famed and erudite pioneer of the form in the early twentieth century, and his collected *Essays in Musical Analysis* remain good to read, even if their style now seems old-fashioned and out of tune with today's musical thinking. Nor are they always accurate. Scholarship has progressed since Tovey's time.

Nevertheless, what Tovey wrote still towers over much of what passes for programme notes today. Even during my own post-Tovey boyhood, programme notes incorporated – as Tovey's did – musical examples because it was assumed that concert-goers could read music. Today, such notes would be branded elitist. To include musical terminology at all tends to be frowned upon. I have been asked why, in my own notes, I employ such terms as 'counterpoint', which nobody understands. But are football correspondents similarly chided for writing 'penalty' or 'free kick'? Somehow I think not. Though I am all against jargon, the use of an established, accessible musical term is preferable to a paragraph of explanation.

Concert programmes are now a dumbed-down art in which fatuous puffs about the performers occupy more space than the notes themselves, and adverts are given more space still. Traditional notes, as the chief executive of a concert organisation has remarked to me, are now 'irrelevant'. In the sense that most concerts today take place in darkened halls, he was perhaps right. But notes are written to be read before and after an event, as well as during it, and this book's intention is to fill that need.

In the sixteen years I spent editing the Edinburgh Festival's programme notes, there were a number of house rules which I worked out with the then Festival director, Peter Diamand, whose European outlook differed from, and was refreshingly less 'commercial' than, the British. Diamand's beliefs, which I shared, were that notes should contain facts rather than flimflam; that speculation was acceptable so long as it was informed; that notes should be coherently devised by a single writer for the contents of a single programme; that connections between one work and another should be mentioned; that the author, as Tovey once decreed, should act as counsel for the defence — Diamand detested notes which gave the impression that 'This is a bad work but let's perform it anyway'; and that artists' biographies should be confined to 150 words, should include no adjectives and should supply no information about what a performer would be performing in future seasons.

Though most of these principles have fallen by the wayside, they are still the ones to which I, as a note-writer, would prefer to adhere. In addition, I would say that, wherever possible, a work's place in musical history needs to be established; that its local connections (if any) should be mentioned; and that the writer has a responsibility to lure the reader into the music.

Some of the notes included in these pages are based on notes originally written for one musical organisation or another, but which have gone through a constant process of change, and which have now been changed yet again to suit the needs of a book about a single great composer. No note, whether for a concert programme or for something more permanent, should be merely 'drawn from stock'. Just as every performance of a work forms a part (however small) of that work's history, so every programme note should reflect the state – and status – of that work at the time the annotator is writing about it. Attitudes alter. Here, in this book, are twenty current attitudes (my own, but also quoting those of others) to twenty works that continue to matter.

Finally, a note on format. Each book begins with a fresh assessment of its subject composer and of the way he is performed at the start of the twenty-first century. Recordings are recommended at the end of each short essay. Books are listed for further reading, and technical terms are explained in a brief glossary.

CONRAD WILSON

Edinburgh, Scotland, and Introbio, Italy, 2005

INTRODUCTION

Think of Brahms and we visualise a man prematurely old, stern, stout, white-haired, broad faced, long-bearded. Even in his fifties, that was pretty much how he looked. Think of Mendelssohn shortly before his death and we still see the teenage composer of the overture to *A Midsummer Night's Dream*. Mozart at the time of *The Magic Flute* and Schubert at the time of *Winterreise* still looked like young men, because that was what they were, even though each of them, like Mendelssohn at 38, was soon to die.

But Brahms, or so we like to think, was never young, and when he died at 63 he looked as if he had lived a very long life. His mission, as he said some years earlier, had been accomplished. His will was signed. No unfinished masterpiece lay on his desk for future scholars and editors to pore over and complete. His third-floor Viennese apartment at 4 Karlsgasse where (in contrast with Beethoven's ever-changing and ever more squalid premises) he had lived from the day of his arrival in that city twenty-six years earlier, was neat and clean, his Streicher grand piano closed, polished, a few books on the lid.

Above the piano, fixed to the wall, was a bust of Beethoven, the composer with whom his name was so often misleadingly associated. On a table, his Viennese coffee machine lay at the ready. In his library, 'the haunt of no mere musician', his scores were tidily shelved. His high desk, at which he stood to compose in the same way as Ernest Hemingway would later write his novels, was uncluttered.

As all this suggests, Brahms lived an orderly life. In the morning, he worked from 7am. He lunched at the Red Hedgehog, his neighbourhood inn. He walked in the afternoon, stopping in a Viennese café to read the papers. In the evening, if he was not going to a concert, or taking part in one, he would work a bit more, write letters, meet friends. He smoked and drank in Gause's beer-hall, prompting Tchaikovsky, in transit from Russia on one occasion, to write: 'I have been on the booze with Brahms'.

So the belief that Brahms was a grump was only partly true; nor was he 'always old'. Arriving a day too soon for his famous, life-changing first meeting with Robert and Clara Schumann in Düsseldorf, he was greeted by one of their daughters, who said her parents were out and spoke later of the slim, good-looking young man with long fair hair who had come to the door. Brahms at 20 was every inch the romantic young German, the eligible bachelor who could play the piano with enough fire to make him shine like a new Liszt.

It was his move to Vienna which transformed him into a middle-aged bourgeois who, as he admitted himself, had missed his opportunity to get married, and felt condemned, if that was the word, to permanent bachelorhood. His deep yet inert relationship with Clara Schumann made the other women in his life seem lightweight, his interest in them for the most part brief.

Clearly he was a clumsy suitor, who found it easier to retreat into solitude, or intellectual discussion, or the company of drinking companions, than to pursue romance in any positive sort of way. Like P. G. Wodehouse's Mr Mulliner, he was more likely to say: 'My eyes today have that unmistakable look, which is to be seen only in the eyes of confirmed bachelors, whose feet have been dragged to the very brink of the pit, and who have gazed at close range into the naked face of matrimony'.

Yet, as a composer, he was persistent enough. Schumann, before sickness of mind intervened, encouraged him to write orchestral music, bringing about the composition of the magisterial First Piano Concerto, the musical turning point in Brahms's career. Hissed at and vilified for some of his most important works – Bernard Shaw, not at all on his wavelength, memorably called him 'the Leviathan maunderer' – he learned how to cope with public contempt in ways which other composers (Schumann included) failed to do, and he lived long enough to win renown. Had he lived even longer, he might have recognised that, far from being a musical reactionary – as Wagner's supporters proclaimed him – he was actually a progressive, as Arnold Schoenberg (a dedicated Wagnerian) was one of the first to recognise.

Brahms's destructive self-criticism, which deprived us of so much music he deemed unfit for performance, at least ensured that the works he allowed to survive were mostly masterpieces. Choosing no more than twenty of them for a book such as this has been no easier than choosing twenty by Mozart or Schubert, who, though they died younger, were infinitely more productive. The vast metamorphoses which some of Brahms's greatest works underwent – from symphony to concerto, piano duo to piano quintet – could be radical; but his labours were rewarded.

The metamorphoses we ourselves chose to put them through were another matter. The big, thick-textured, bottom-heavy performances of Brahms given in outsize concert halls in the second half of the twentieth century were more often than not distortions of the truth. Brahms, though not opposed to big orchestras, preferred smaller ones, such as the Meiningen Court Orchestra, which clarified the fine detail of his music and sharpened its rhythms. People like Herbert von Karajan were very bad for Brahms, just as Sir Charles Mackerras has been very good for him. It's a belated lesson, but one which has been worth learning.

Johannes Brahms was born in 1833 in a shabby timbered tenement in Hamburg, later destroyed at the height of the Second World War. His father was a kindly, reputedly humorous musician, who played the double bass and flugelhorn and was seventeen years younger than his first wife (and eighteen years older, it might be added, than his second, who in 1866 became the 33-year-old composer's stepmother).

Impoverished though it was, young Brahms's home life was happy. His father gave him music lessons, but a proposed American tour for him as a boy wonder was clearly a non-starter — Brahms and his father were by no means another Wolfgang and Leopold Mozart. Before long, the boy found his niche as a tavern pianist, a job from which he made his escape with the aid of the Hungarian violinist Eduard Remenyi.

From Remenyi, he learned about Hungarian gypsy music, a useful attribute and major influence on his style, as things turned out. On tour together, they visited Joseph Joachim, the second and even more influential violinist in Brahms's life. Joachim was impressed enough with him to organise introductions to Liszt and Schumann. His meeting with the latter in 1853 famously bore more fruit than that with the former.

When Schumann's mental illness in 1854 destroyed their plans to work together, Brahms took a post in Detmold, where for three months each year he taught piano, conducted a chorus and walked in the countryside. But Hamburg, where he had another chorus, remained his home until his decision to follow Beethoven's footsteps to Vienna in 1863. There, his temporary appointment as conductor of the Vienna

Singakademie gave him the toehold he needed. In 1865, he composed his German Requiem, partly in memory of his mother, and he was on his way.

One

1854
PIANO TRIO IN B MAJOR, OP. 8

Allegro con brio   Scherzo: Allegro molto   Adagio   Allegro

Mozart was 19 when genius, in the form of his G major Violin Concerto, first struck. Officially it was his 216th work, its predecessors being the products of a prolific, immensely talented *wunderkind*. Mendelssohn, however, outstripped him by composing, at 16, his inspired Octet for strings, having previously displayed his precocity in an array of pieces more phenomenal than any by Mozart at a similar age. But Brahms, traditionally considered a plodder, was all of 20 before he produced his first masterpiece, the Piano Trio in B major, Op. 8, stamping his credentials upon it in the form of a sublime, utterly Brahmsian opening theme. Later, he confused the issue by revising the work so thoroughly that it bore only fleeting resemblances to the music he first wrote. The opening theme, however, remained just as it was, because Brahms knew he could not improve upon it.

Writing to his confidante Clara Schumann about his decision to revise the work thirty-five years after composing it, Brahms remarked with typical dolefulness: 'It will not be so dreary as before, but will it be any better?' Considering Brahms's penchant for destroying any piece of chamber music that displeased him, we are lucky to have both versions of what was supposedly the first of his three authorised trios for piano, violin and cello (there were almost certainly earlier ones, including a mysterious, rather fine work in A major, attributed to Brahms, which came to light in 1924). Neither version is in any way dreary, yet his question to Clara Schumann was nevertheless worth asking. In its originally published form, the B major Trio was an established, greatly admired though admittedly imperfect, youthful masterpiece when Brahms's publishers gave him the opportunity to rethink it.

For someone like Brahms, it was an irresistible offer, which prompted him to decide that the music called for radical rather than cosmetic surgery. But there was a paradox in the result, which was that in perfecting the original score he jettisoned so much of it that it ceased to be the work he had previously written. This was much more than the Brahmsian equivalent of what Wagner did to *Tannhäuser* (or Verdi to *Macbeth*) at a later stage in his career. Overnight, his first piano trio had suddenly become his last, a mature, sometimes stern work in his profound 'late' manner. What performers today have at their disposal, therefore, are two largely different pieces, each of which happens to have the same opus number, the same key and the same magnificent, instantly memorable opening theme. Which to choose?

The choice, for most performers, seems not to be difficult. The original version is now treated, somewhat unfairly, more as a curiosity than a masterpiece. Almost everybody opts for the second, infinitely terser and tidier version, even if what they are playing is no longer the work which Brahms had composed in 1854 in the shadow of his friend Robert Schumann's attempted suicide and subsequent madness. By 1889, Brahms had moved on, and what he produced in that year was a scrupulously structured, carefully calculated, perfectly poised masterpiece, rather than the messily spontaneous one which had originally been described as 'wild'. But it was wise of him to recognise that it still needed its original opening theme.

That theme, though he was only 20 when he wrote it, is one of the longest, grandest and most memorable he ever produced, and in 1889, as in 1854, he knew exactly what to do with it. The piano launches it, the cello joins in, the violin supplies lift-off and the movement is on its way. Where it is going depends on which version of the work is being performed, but in the revision its progress is as inexorable as the theme itself.

The compact scherzo, which follows, is the one movement Brahms saw no need to alter drastically. In its gossamer delicacy and *leggiero* piano writing, the music sounds like a tribute to Mendelssohn, perhaps even to Schumann, with touches of Schubert in the piano's crystalline upper register; but the waltz which forms the slower-moving central section is of the choicest Brahmsian sort.

At the start of the contemplative, austerely lovely slow movement, piano tone and string tone are contrasted with each other until eventually they mesh. The finale exudes ferocious minor-key agitation and urgency within the framework of a rondo, offset by a vibrant theme in D major which is one of the high inspirations of Brahms's revision of the music.

In both versions of the work, memories of Schumann — whether immediate or distilled — lurk in the music. Though the unmarried Brahms, for much of his life, was closely involved with Clara Schumann, there is no doubt that Robert Schumann's incarceration in an asylum, far from being privately welcome, affected him deeply. Schumann was his friend and mentor, someone whose musical advice was important to him, and with whom he had been longing to work on various projects. This opportunity was now denied him. As a result, 1854 was a year of genuine grief, which by 1889 had changed to increasing awareness of his own mortality.

Though most recordings of Brahms's B major Trio are of his 1889 revision of the score, an ensemble aptly called the Trio Opus Eight, with Michael Hauber as pianist, performs both versions, at bargain price, in a highly desirable two-disc set which additionally includes the two later piano trios, Op. 87 and 101. The persuasive players owe their name to the fact that they were studying Brahms's early trio at the time they established themselves in 1985 (Arte Nova Dig. 74321 51641-2).

Among several excellent performances of Brahms's perfected Op. 8, the Florestan Trio's stands out for its translucence, intimacy and fine detail, with the Edinburgh-born pianist Susan Tomes as pivot. This, too, comes as part of a two-disc set, in which four other works — the Horn Trio, Op. 40, the Clarinet Trio, Op. 114 and the rest of the piano trios — make this a superb introduction to Brahms's piano-based chamber music (Hyperion CDA67251/2)

But the Florestans (who call themselves after one side, the musically more outgoing side, of Schumann's split personality) do not stand alone. The Chung Trio, with Kyung-Wha Chung as violinist, Myung-Wha Chung as cellist and Myung Whun Chung as pianist, bring keen family rapport to a beautifully nuanced account of Op. 8 with Op. 87 as coupling (Decca 421 425-2). Augustin Dumay, Jian Wang and Maria João Pires are certainly no family, but they show how France, China and Portugal can constructively converge in fine, romantic performances of the same two trios (DG 447 055 2GH).

Two

1858
PIANO CONCERTO NO. 1 IN D MINOR, OP. 15

Maestoso   Adagio   Rondo: Allegro non troppo

By any standards, Brahms's First Piano Concerto is an astounding feat for a composer of 25. Compared with it, Beethoven's B flat major Piano Concerto, completed at the same age, is a lightweight prentice piece. It is against the epic scale of the 'Eroica' symphony, completed at 34, that Brahms's precocious masterpiece needs to be measured – and only the most dedicated anti-Brahmsian would find it seriously wanting. Its opening flourish is no mere classical fanfare but something both searing and transfixing. A harshly vehement melody for the strings, a threatening roll on the kettledrums, a darkly rocking rhythm and a use of double trills so emphatic that they sound like alarm bells (especially when the piano later plays them) combine to make the first notes of the first movement heave with rage.

The story that they reflect young Brahms's reactions to Schumann's attempted suicide in the Rhine may or may not be true, yet on the evidence of such musical fist-shaking there seems little reason to doubt it. The entire work, indeed, is like a running commentary on Brahms's relationship with the Schumanns, both Robert and Clara, at the time of Robert's mental decline and death in 1856. The very dates of the composition – begun in 1854, soon after Brahms had first met the husband and wife who would so influence his career, but not completed until almost five years later, when he had become linked with the widowed Clara as with no other woman in his life – imply some form of musical autobiography.

Yet, Brahms being the abstract composer he was, the work's genesis has more to do with its structural complexities than with imagery or events. For a start, the music he began to write in 1854 was not his D minor Piano Concerto – whatever his ambitions as a pianist-composer – but a four-movement sonata for two pianos employing material from an abandoned symphony. The key, like that of the future concerto, was D minor, but the two works otherwise appear to have had little in common. Moreover, by the time he started writing the finale of the sonata, Brahms said he needed more than two pianos to do justice to his conception.

Even at this point, however, he was not yet heading towards a piano concerto. The sonata, he decided, would have to be transformed back into a symphony, and in this form the first movement was duly completed. But composition once more ground to a halt, and it was only then that the idea of a concerto entered his mind. From 1856 until 1858, the project underwent massive restructuring. The sonata's slow movement, jettisoned from the concerto, ended up as the inexorable 'All Flesh is as Grass' funeral march in the *German Requiem*. Another movement was destroyed. But with advice from friends, including Clara Schumann, on the subject of the closing rondo, the concerto gradually gained its perfected shape.

Its slow movement, with the Latin inscription 'Benedictus qui vent in Nimine Domini' written over the main theme, was reputedly drawn from sketches for a projected Mass – a further link, according to Brahms's violinist friend Joseph Joachim, with Schumann's sad demise. The music nevertheless remained sternly symphonic in conception, as the Second Piano Concerto and the Violin Concerto would also do when Brahms came to write them during the next decade.

Though the keyboard part proved formidably difficult, the work was no mere virtuoso showpiece. Brains were needed for its performance as well as brawn. Brahms, as soloist, supplied both attributes at the premiere, which Joachim conducted in Hanover in January 1859. The audience was by no means bowled over, but was at least not hostile, as Leipzig's listeners proved to be during the second performance five days later. The Gewandhaus Orchestra's indifference to the music, and the hisses at the end of the performance, were an inglorious moment in Leipzig history.

Yet the critics who dismissed the work as a symphony with piano obbligato were not imperceptive. Their mistake was to diagnose this as a shortcoming rather than a virtue of the concerto, which has been more accurately assessed in our own time as a statement of ideas combined with commentaries on them. Just as much as in Liszt and Wagner, the music – particularly the vast first movement – is about thematic transformation and about how a soft answer can turn away wrath. Given the black balefulness of the orchestral introduction, the piano's entry is remarkably self-contained, and the soloist's subsequent presentation of a romantic new theme is an example of Brahms at his most glowingly lyrical.

The major-key *adagio*, employing the same rocking metre as the first movement but subtly slowing it down, sustains this lyrical mood. Whether it is about Schumann's death or about Brahms's feelings for Clara we shall never know, but it is music of profoundly Brahmsian beauty in which piano and orchestra for the most part converse serenely with each other. Yet emotion is an underlying presence, and a central section discloses moody minor-key leanings. The music reaches a rapt climax for the soloist followed by an orchestral postlude in which the unexpected strains of a solo viola are briefly heard.

The vigorous final rondo sounds like Brahms's response to two previous concerto finales – those of Mozart's K466 in the same key and of Beethoven's Piano Concerto No. 3 in C minor. Both these works, after minor-key sombreness, suddenly end in major-key joviality, and the same happens in the Brahms. Yet in none of them does a happy ending trivialise what has gone before, nor does Brahms's insertion of a catlike fugue seem in any sense a copy of the fugue inserted by Beethoven in his finale at almost the same point.

Alfred Brendel's devotion to this work, dating from the period which he considers to include Brahms's most beautiful and Schumannesque music, is a subject touched upon in his wonderful conversation book, *The Veil of Order*. The piano writing, he claims, is much clearer and more distinctly laid out than in the later works, 'where one easily gets stuck in those inner and subsidiary parts, and asks oneself why Brahms does not equip the pianist with eleven or twelve fingers'.

The authority of his recorded performance, with Claudio Abbado and the Berlin Philharmonic, bears this out, making it a primary choice among the many versions of this work available on disc. It can be bought on its own (Philips 420 071-2) or as part of a collection including the Second Piano Concerto, the Four Ballades and the piano transcription of the theme and variations from the Sextet No. 1 for strings. The ballades and sextet date from the period Brendel so admires; the concerto does not, and in his book he confesses a lack of enthusiasm for it, though one would not guess this from the quality of his performance (Philips 446 925-2).

Though Stephen Kovacevich on EMI and Emil Gilels on DG also give masterly accounts of this work, there is a purity and nervous tension in Sir Clifford Curzon's old recording with George Szell as conductor which places it in a class of its own. Listen to it, and be enthralled (Decca Legends 466 376-2DM).

Three

1860
STRING SEXTET IN B FLAT MAJOR, OP. 18

Allegro ma non troppo   Andante, ma moderato

Scherzo: Allegro molto   Rondo: Poco allegretto e grazioso

Brahms composed the first of his two string sextets at a watershed in his life. Though born in nordic Hamburg and for a time usefully employed as a conductor and teacher in Detmold, he yearned for the south and might have settled in Italy had he not found Vienna to be a congenial compromise. The city which had housed Haydn, Mozart, Beethoven and Schubert possessed an inspirational musical history, a sympathetic local critic (Eduard Hanslick, who was less sympathetic to Wagner and his 'music of the future') and a proximity to lakes and mountains. Seldom a fast operator, Brahms waited nine years after his first exploratory visit to the city in 1862 before settling there permanently. By then he had completed his two sextets, each of them scored for two violins, two violas and two cellos, though only the second of these works was written in Vienna itself.

Yet both of them could be said to have a Viennese accent, the first sounding positively Schubertian in the unhurried discursiveness of its finale and in the important role bestowed (as in Schubert's string quintet) on the principal cello. It was the first piece of chamber music for strings which Brahms deemed worthy of an opus number, even if, in a letter, he dismissed it as trash. And it was composed at a time of emotional turmoil, when his suppressed love for Clara Schumann was temporarily supplanted by his engagement to Agathe von Siebold, a young soprano who inspired several of his songs. Brahms's reputation as a grump has always found favour with those who dislike his music, but his two sextets – glowing products of his prentice years – tell a different story.

The opening of the B flat major Sextet is an early manifestation of his ability – one of his great abilities – to launch a work as if it were in glorious mid-flow. The swaying main theme sets the tone, its waltz-like pulse sustained by a warm and almost unwavering momentum, with only an occasional clouding of its euphonious progress.

Then, in the slow movement, the colours passionately darken, the mellowness of the home key changing here to the powerful D minor of his First Piano Concerto. Not for nothing did Louis Malle choose this movement to accompany the famous love scene in his film *Les Amants*, odd though this may seem to people who claim to find Brahms's music detumescent. But then, this is a movement uniquely gripping in the way in which it develops what seems to be an austerely Bachian theme and variations into what, in Brahmsian terms, proves increasingly romantic and intense, its textures powerfully underpinned by the two cellos, its atmosphere dominated by each varied repetition of the memorable, ever-present theme.

The scherzo, in comparison, is brief, rustic, slightly Beethovenian, its runaway central section contrasting with its otherwise rather clodhopping rhythm, recalling Wagner's rude description of Brahms as resembling Mendelssohn and Schumann swaddled in leather. But the radiant sweetness of the finale dispels such notions with the help of a beautiful, easy-going main theme which is put through various transformations before the movement, with a sudden burst of speed, spurts joyfully to its close.

But in one sense perhaps not quite its close. Brahms had more to say via the combined voices of a string sextet, but waited five years before saying it in his G major Sextet, Op. 36. Famed for his afterthoughts, he had a penchant for composing works in pairs – the cello sonatas, the clarinet sonatas, the first two string quartets, the serenades, the piano concertos – in such a way that the second could seem the obverse of, or a continuation of, the first. Between the two sextets there is certainly such a link, even if some listeners claim that the second is so much more mature than the first that comparison is pointless.

For others, however, the connections seem so obvious, and so fascinating, that it is hard to consider one of these works without reference to the other. Together they add up to – or would do, if their composer were other than Brahms – what sound like a series of episodes in the life of an artist. But coming from someone who shunned descriptive music, who never wrote an opera and whose *Tragic* overture depicted a wholly abstract tragedy, the music can hardly be expected to tell us anything too specific about what Brahms had on his mind in the year 1865, what books he was reading, what subjects he was attracted to. Brahms never composed a *Transfigured Night*, though in the slow movement of his earlier sextet he surely came quite close in spirit to Schoenberg's romantically descriptive masterpiece for the same forces (and it was the astute Schoenberg, we should remember, who recognised this reputedly backward-looking composer as 'Brahms the Progressive').

In his Second Sextet, he provided further hints of such capabilities. A recognisable narrative thread may be absent, but ciphers of the sort employed by Schumann when he wanted to convey secret messages to his wife are undeniably present. Brahms, too, wanted to convey secret messages to Schumann's wife – now for some years his widow – and what better way than to employ methods used by her husband?

When Brahms started work on his Second Sextet, he was apparently still in the same emotional turmoil, if such a word is not too strong to use of Brahms, as when composing the first. Though eternally devoted, on various levels, to Clara Schumann, he had not yet forgotten Agathe von Siebold, the young soprano to whom he had been engaged. Enshrined in the music are his memories of Agathe as well as the state of his feelings about Clara. The letters of Agathe's name (AGAHE in German musical nomenclature, AGABE in British) form the passionate climax of the first movement's second subject, suggesting that she still mattered to him.

The composer himself put it strongly enough when he said of this passage in the music: 'Here is where I tore myself free from my last love.' A work containing not only this but also self-confessed references to Clara — in the rising motif at the start of the same movement, and in the similarly rising motif (written ten years earlier) which yearningly opens the slow movement and reappears in the finale – can only be called autobiographical, however improbable this may seem in music by Brahms.

It is certainly a more complex and cryptic work than the First Sextet, reminding us that Karl Geiringer's famous description of the composer as 'Brahms the Ambiguous' supplied a sharper picture of his contradictory personality than most comments of its kind. The G minor scherzo which forms the second movement is more of an anti-scherzo, rather too slow and rather too serious to justify the title, though its stamping trio section is jovial enough. In the F minor theme and variations which form the *adagio*, the mood is initially restrained and sad, but soon erupts with what sounds almost like anger. As in the previous sextet, the music is both romantic and grandly baroque. The finale goes through its paces with a sort of tremulous vitality which manages to bring the work to its close in a state of what sounds something like happiness.

Among recordings of Brahms's sextets, those by the British-based Raphael Ensemble catch the spirit of the music to admiration. The sound is warm, clear, balanced and intimate enough to suggest that these are genuine chamber performances rather than statements delivered to a big audience in a big concert hall (Hyperion CDA66276).

Four

1864
LIEDER UND GESÄNGE, OP. 32

1. 'Wie rafft' ich mich auf in der Nacht' (August Graf von Platen)
2. 'Nicht mehr zu dir zu gehen' (folk song from the Vltava)
3. 'Ich schleich' umher' (August Graf von Platen)
4. 'Der Strom, der neben mir verrauschte' (August Graf von Platen)
5. 'Wehe, so willst du mich wieder' (August Graf von Platen)
6. 'Du sprichst, das ich mich tauschte' (August Graf von Platen)
7. 'Bitteres zu sagen denkst du' (Georg Friedrich Daumer)
8. 'So stehn wir, ich und meine Weide' (Georg Friedrich Daumer)
9. 'Wie bist du, meine Königin' (Georg Friedrich Daumer)

Brahms composed about 200 songs, mostly gathered into groups and identified simply by opus numbers and first lines. Descriptive names, such as *Magelone-Lieder* for the set of fifteen songs, Op. 33, were rare – or rarer, at any rate, than in Schumann or Schubert. For the most part, Brahms was content to provide a generalised identity tag, with *Lieder und Gesänge* (which he employed five times in the course of his career) as his top favourite. Since this, in essence, means merely 'Songs and Songs', it is not greatly enlightening, though by implication there is a shade of difference between *Lieder* (meaning, by common acceptance, 'German art songs') and *Gesänge* (meaning, simply, 'songs'). So when the customarily laconic composer went so far as to describe his eight songs, Op. 14, as *Lieder und Romanzen*, this must have been a major statement from a man who more often than not stuck to the purely numerical *Vier Gesänge* ('Four Songs'), *Sieben Lieder* ('Seven Songs') and so forth.

But the nine *Lieder und Gesänge*, Op. 32, are more than just 'songs and songs'. They are actually a disguised song cycle, with an essential running order and a definite subject, however modest about it was the composer himself. Without a shadow of doubt, these are passionate love songs (a fact which would not in itself bind them into a cycle); but they are also something significantly more than that. They are about the progress, or lack of progress, of an unhappy relationship, voiced through the words of two different poets, and it is clear that the bitterly suffering narrator is the 31-year-old Brahms himself.

Performed separately, as they often are, the songs provide no more than a glimpse of their sombre and lonely ardour. Heard as an entity, they relate, as one authority has put it, 'a story of lost love, remorse and undying fidelity'. Their unnamed addressee, as almost always with Brahms, could only have been Clara Schumann, fourteen years his senior

(Brahms's mother, it may be worth repeating, was seventeen years older than his father) and by that time Robert Schumann's widow.

From the opening song, in which the singer trudges desolately through the streets of a dark town in a manner suggestive of Schubert's *Winterreise*, to the sweet ruefulness of the adoring final tribute to the distant beloved, the message is unmistakable. But the last song, deservedly famous out of context, really does need to be heard as the resigned and eloquent outcome of its eight predecessors. Brahms would later write many more songs for Clara, though none more touching than this.

'Last' songs, whatever their context, mattered much to a composer of Brahms's disposition. The last three in this particular cycle were all settings of poems by Georg Friedrich Daumer, a homeopathic doctor, translator, Rosicrucian and author of many of the verses Brahms poured into his beguiling *Liebeslieder* waltzes. Though Brahms was peculiarly partial to Daumer's work, the poet did not return the admiration. On the single occasion the two men met, he claimed never to have heard of Johannes Brahms. Yet it is with Brahms that his name is now solely and inseparably linked.

The last songs of all — though here we are leaping forward in the life of a composer who was in some ways old at 31 to a composer who was infinitely older at 63 — were the *Four Serious Songs*, Op. 121, which he wrote in 1896, the year before his death. By then, almost all other forms of composition had ceased, and his last will, the so-called 'Ischl Testament', had been signed. The final orchestral work, the Double Concerto for violin and cello, was already a thing of the past, completed nine years earlier in 1887. The two valedictory clarinet sonatas had followed in 1894, along with the very different, greatly charming, positively lightweight *German Folksongs* in seven volumes. Only the eleven deeply spiritual *Chorale Preludes* for organ, Op. 122, remained to be written.

In the *Four Serious Songs*, it has been said, Brahms came closer than in any other work to the level of stress to be found in Mahler. Perhaps in parts of his *German Requiem* he came even closer, especially in performances – such as Daniel Barenboim's – which probe the doom-laden sombreness of the 'All Flesh is as Grass' funeral march rather than the life-force behind the death-consciousness of the work. In neither case, however, did he sufficiently lose grip of his own stoicism to seem a premature purveyor of Mahlerish angst.

Yet, if the *Four Serious Songs*, as used to be said, were to be sung by anyone other than a sepulchral bass, or bass-baritone such as Hans Hotter, then only Kathleen Ferrier would fill the bill. Music of such breadth of expression, such gloomy power, such relentless pain required the integrity of a genuine deep contralto voice, containing not a chink of light such as might be supplied inadvertently by a mere mezzo. Today, the music's message that everything is transitory has come to seem less exclusively the property of a certain sort of singer, and its elegiac beauty – inspired by what Brahms correctly perceived to be the imminent demise of Clara Schumann, who had just suffered a stroke – to be more 'philosophical' than directly or threateningly Biblical.

With typically feigned modesty, Brahms himself dismissed the result as a 'trifle', the songs not only 'un-Christian' but also 'godless harvester's revels'. By an irony he must have appreciated, however, he finished them on 7 May 1896, his 63rd birthday. Clara died a fortnight later, and Brahms did not live to be 64. Far from being trifling, the music stood darkly apart from the rest of his output of songs, the music inspiring Sir Malcolm Sargent to orchestrate the piano accompaniments in a manner, so the conductor arrogantly considered, to be more appropriate to their solemn mien. No doubt Sargent wanted to prove that they belonged to the special world of the *German Requiem*, the *Alto Rhapsody* and the *Song of Destiny* rather than that of Brahms's large quantity of more varied lieder.

Those already aware of Brahms's ambivalent sense of religious belief can certainly find evidence of it here. Though the words are Biblical – the first three songs are drawn from Ecclesiastes, the fourth from Corinthians – the music treats them as literature, and it is in that vein that we should listen to them. Though they have been said to form a pocket requiem, they simply represent Brahms's awareness of his own mortality and that of some by then absent friends.

The funereal pulse of the opening song, the pure pessimism of the second, the flashbacks to the Fourth Symphony in the third, and the consolation of the final song certainly add up to a unity, though whether they represent the swansong of the German *Lied* – as used to be claimed – is another matter. Mahler, after all, had yet to write his *Rückert Lieder*.

Of the nine Op. 32 songs, the gifted Thomas Quasthoff has become today's most apt and heartfelt interpreter. His disc, with piano accompaniments of the utmost sensitivity from Justus Zeyen, is made even more desirable through the inclusion of two other fine Brahms song sets, Op. 72 and Op. 94, and some magnificent Liszt (DG 463 183-2). In contrast, and no less desirable, is Jessye Norman's two-disc set of Brahms's so-called women's songs, with Daniel Barenboim as accompanist (DG 459 469-2).

Anne Sofie von Otter's Brahms recital, including the two exquisite songs, Op. 91, with viola obbligato, is greatly winning (DG 429 727-2), though this is hardly the word for Brigitte Fassbaender's starkly, not to say shatteringly, dramatic declamation of the *Four Serious Songs* with Elisabeth Leonskaja, a performance in a class of its own. More Brahms, and Schumann's Op. 31 *Liederkreis* songs, complete this obligatory disc (Teldec 9031-74872-2).

Five

1864
PIANO QUINTET IN F MINOR, OP. 34

Allegro non troppo   Andante, un poco adagio   Scherzo: Allegro

Finale: Poco sostenuto – Allegro non troppo

'You may place a picture on the title-page, namely a head – with a pistol in front of it. That will give you some idea of the music. I shall send you a photograph of myself for the purpose.' Brahms's famously dolorous words to his publisher in 1875 concerned a piano quartet he had composed twenty years earlier but remained dissatisfied with. They summed up his attitude to much of his chamber music, vast amounts of which he destroyed, sometimes before anyone performed it, sometimes after. Of his estimated twenty-or-so string quartets, only three survive. Just think if Beethoven had indulged in such musical infanticide! Other works escaped with revision, often radical, over a period of many years.

Nobody should be surprised, therefore, that Brahms's Piano Quintet in F minor, Op. 34, was composed first as a string quintet and then as a sonata for two pianos before emerging in its final form as a masterpiece for piano and strings. What was unusual was that there was a gap of only two years between the first and last versions of the work, suggesting that this was music which Brahms was determined to get right as soon as he could, and that he definitely knew when he had done so.

In its original string quintet form, its richness of sonority challenged even a violinist as resourceful as the great Joseph Joachim, who complained in 1862 that the music 'lacked charm' and advised the young composer to consider rewriting it for piano. Brahms, rewriting it for two pianos, retained the original richness of texture and was so pleased with the result, when he performed it with the brilliant Carl Tausig in 1864, that he was actually confident enough to say so to his publisher.

The absence of string tone, on the other hand, displeased his friend and adviser Clara Schumann, who suggested that a version for piano and strings might be the solution. Not, she added, that she had anything against the original string quintet version, which she had hailed as 'one long melody from start to finish'. But, in the words of one pianist to another, she considered that the piano sonata, with its ideas 'scattered as generously as if from a cornucopia', required to be reassembled.

The composer, for once undaunted, remained happy enough with the sonata to publish it separately as Op. 34b, in which form it remains a splendid, though sadly neglected, work. Ten years or more before tackling his first two symphonies, he had begun to achieve his own special sound-world and recognisable style of melody. There is no doubt, however, that in its final version for piano and strings – as Clara Schumann astutely surmised – the music possesses exactly the right balance of richness, clarity and contrast.

Sir Donald Tovey, Edinburgh University's celebrated author of *Essays in Musical Analysis*, called the first movement of the piano quintet 'powerfully tragic', a description he used more than once about Brahms. But minor keys, even when it is Brahms who is employing them, do not necessarily imply tragedy, and today we might prefer to call the music tempestuous, sinewy or virile. True, the quiet first statement of the main theme on violin, cello and piano, playing in octaves and 'undistorted by harmony', sounds almost hesitant, but that is so as to make the second statement, with the strings playing fortissimo against the piano's plunging arpeggios, seem all the more ringingly magnificent. Its breadth of utterance, moreover, provides immediate evidence that a substantial, imposingly structured masterpiece lies ahead.

The softly lapping *andante* in A flat major – its main theme a deliberate reminiscence of a slow song from Schubert's *Die schöne Müllerin* cycle – is a sustained, lilting lullaby which pours balm on the storms and stresses of the previous movement. But in the scherzo, one of Brahms's very best, tension returns via a syncopated melody which swells out of the introductory soft pizzicato throb of the cello at the bottom of its register. The key is now an ominous C minor, the mood fierce and relentless until the central trio section brings out the sunshine in buoyant C major.

After a repeat of the scherzo's C minor thunder, the finale begins slowly and gropingly in mysteriously harmonised tones that provide the most melancholy moments in the entire work. But when the main *allegro* section arrives, the air clears and the cello and piano launch a whimsical little march which Brahms himself, it is said, performed with more deliberation than most modern performers. Later, the speed excitably increases to *presto non troppo* and the time alters to six-in-a-bar for a whirling, pounding coda. For all its vivacity, however, this large closing section has sufficient integrity to bring the work to its end in the original dark key of F minor and not, as might have been expected, in the glow of F major.

Brahms's Piano Quintet is a big work which thrives on big performances, but it is not a symphony. Its gently lapping slow movement must sound like the chamber music it is, and the rest of a performance requires to be in proportion. Maurizio Pollini, in his recording with the Quartetto Italiano, achieves this feat of balance in a performance which never suffers from the bottom-heaviness to which this work is prone. If the music sounds hard-driven, it is always to some purpose, and the slumbrous slow movement in contrast sounds all the more effective because of this (DG 419 673-2).

A similar vitality courses through Sir Clifford Curzon's much older recording with the Amadeus Quartet, which has all the nervous energy to be expected of a live performance from this captivatingly unpredictable and intelligent pianist. Though London's Royal Festival Hall was not the most acoustically helpful environment for a performer of Curzon's private tensions, or for the Viennese warmth of the Amadeus's string tone, it clearly contributed to the risk-taking excitement of the performance. With Schubert's 'Trout' quintet, a Curzon favourite, as coupling, this BBC relic of the 1970s has been well worth preserving (BBC Legends BBCL4009-2).

Six

1865
TRIO FOR HORN, VIOLIN AND PIANO IN
E FLAT MAJOR, OP. 40

Andante   Scherzo: Allegro

Adagio mesto   Finale: Allegro con brio

Brahms's *German Requiem* was not his only elegy for his mother, whose death from a stroke in February 1865 cast its shadow over much of what he composed that year. But whereas the writing of the requiem took ages (even by Brahms's unhurried standards) to reach its final form – at the outset it had been planned as a memorial to Schumann, who died in 1856 – much less time was required to produce the similarly valedictory, and by no means insubstantial, Horn Trio in E flat, Op. 40.

As with the later, similarly rueful Clarinet Trio, the employment of a wind instrument – especially a wind instrument with a distinctively Brahmsian tone quality – served as conduit for the melancholy, reflective side of his personality. In the Horn Trio, the result was music of grave, autumnal beauty, not at all suggestive of a composer who was still in his early thirties when he completed it at Lichtental, near Baden-Baden, a spa town which had become one of his favourite retreats. There, each summer, he could compose and meet friends, not least Clara Schumann, who lived there in her widowhood.

By May 1865, just four months after his mother's death, he had completed his trio in her memory. Breaking with classical form, which he had hitherto largely respected, he reverted here to something more baroque, and produced a Bachian structure with four movements in slow-quick-slow-quick layout. Bach, whom he revered, had been much on his mind. A friend, dropping in on him in his rooms in Vienna (by then his adopted city) after his return from his mother's funeral in Hamburg, found him sitting at the piano, playing Bach with tears pouring down his cheeks. And with that composer as precedent, he seized his opportunity to incorporate not one but two expressive slow movements in his memorial trio, composing them before the rest of the work.

The second of these, marked *adagio mesto*, was directly concerned with his mother (*mesto* meaning 'mourning'), and its spirit of bitter desolation proved very different from the melodious tenderness and nostalgia of the opening *andante*. But then, the songlike main theme of that opening movement dated from before the death of Christiana Brahms and had been inspired by something else entirely. As the composer himself explained, the music had come to him while he was walking in the Black Forest – 'on the wooded heights above the fir trees' – during a Lichtental holiday the previous year.

Choosing a horn to portray the idyllic forest scene was a poetic masterstroke heightened by the fact that the horn he had in mind was a *Waldhorn* (literally 'forest horn'), a valveless 'natural' horn of a sort that had powerful childhood memories for him. It was the instrument his father played, and which he himself had learned under his father's guidance. Though today the music is usually played on a modern valve horn, Brahms never concealed his characteristic preference for the more archaic instrument. Yet the actual sound of this slow opening movement is richly romantic rather than neo-baroque.

The succeeding scherzo adds some vigorous hunting-horn rusticity to the gentle forest murmurs of the first movement, but the minor-key middle section has a sad lilt clearly pointing towards the great *adagio* which forms the emotional core of the work. Here, the horn tone gains a haunting, sometimes almost Mahlerish eloquence; but the points of climax, with their yearning violin, are pure Brahms. Though Clara Schumann called it 'hard to understand on first hearing', its message seems clear enough.

So is the message of the finale, which develops the hunting element of the scherzo into something more consistently jovial. Darker emotions, at any rate, are kept at bay, but the emotion of the *adagio* is counterbalanced rather than swept aside.

The best and most authentic recording of Brahms's Horn Trio, bearing in mind the composer's preference for a valveless horn, is Andrew Clark's, for the simple reason that he employs a genuine *Waldhorn* to brilliant but poetic effect. Horn works by Beethoven and Mozart fill out the disc (EMI Debut 5 72822-2).

The sound of a modern horn is not to be despised in other recordings, such as the Nash Ensemble's with the F minor Piano Quintet as coupling (CRD 3489), or the Danish Horn Trio's with Ligeti's Brahms-inspired Horn Trio as a fascinating obverse (Chandos 9964). Note, too, that the Florestan Trio's two-disc compilation of Brahms trios includes an outstanding performance of this work featuring Stephen Stirling (Hyperion CDA67251/2).

Seven

1869
LIEBESLIEDER WALTZES, OP. 52

If Brahms had a lighter side – and he undoubtedly did – then here is the sparkling proof of it. *Liebeslieder* means 'love songs', and the eighteen that form his Op. 52 (a further fifteen came five years later) are delectable specimens of their kind – pithy, roguish and written in Viennese waltz-time with none of the soul-searching that went into so many of his more serious songs.

Their scoring, for four voices and four-handed piano accompaniment, suggests them to be intimate in vein – 'a refined apotheosis of domestic music-making', as one authority has put it – and thus not too difficult to sing or play as an after-supper entertainment. But their special appeal to experienced performers – Benjamin Britten once famously presented them at the Aldeburgh Festival with Claudio Arrau as fellow pianist and Heather Harper, Janet Baker, Peter Pears and Thomas Hemsley as soloists – lies in the charm, subtlety and verve that can be brought to them.

The question, if it does not seem too serious to ask it, lies in why Brahms wrote them in the first place, and who or what inspired them. Different biographers have provided different answers. Some say quite accurately that he composed them for Robert and Clara Schumann's beautiful but fragile daughter Julie, with whom he was furtively and dreamily in love before she suddenly announced her engagement to the Italian Count Vittorio Radicati di Marmorito.

When Clara informed the 36-year-old composer of this, with seemingly only the faintest perception of his feelings for Julie, she said that he 'choked and ran from the house'. Yet, since Brahms was bound to have been aware that Julie was dying of tuberculosis, there was clearly an element of fantasy about his unspoken love for her.

With his customary stoicism, however, he moved on from amorous waltzes to what he described as their 'sequel' – the anguished and haunting music of his *Alto Rhapsody*, written in memory of what might have been. The music provides clues to his solitary, romantically repressed personality. Its words consist of three verses from Goethe's *Harzreise im Winter*, which – shades of Schubert's *Winterreise* – tells of a winter journey taken by Goethe in the Harz Mountains in order to recuperate from a broken love affair. Brahms said sarcastically that the melancholy, ultimately supplicatory beauty of his *Alto Rhapsody* represented his 'Bridal Song', and he told Clara

– for whom his feelings were deeper and more enduring – that he did 'this sort of thing with concealed wrath, with rage'. Two years later, in 1872, Julie died.

Whether or not the *Liebeslieder* waltzes form a portrait of Julie before Brahms learned that she was not available, other theories about these love songs are purely musical. According to one commentator, they are Brahms's celebration of a Schubertian heritage, and form part of a 'Schubert project' that preoccupied him during his first ten years in Vienna. From this period date the North German intruder's editions of some of Schubert's unpublished Viennese *Ländler* (precursors of the Strauss waltz) for solo piano; and the links between these pieces and Brahms's piano arrangements of his own *Liebeslieder* waltzes are easy to spot.

But there is yet another factor in the background inspiration for Brahms's *Liebeslieder* waltzes, and that is their Hungarian element, quickly audible in the second song. Like Haydn and Schubert before him, and like his contemporary Johann Strauss (the strains of whose recently composed *Blue Danube*, music of which he was specially fond, lurk in the ninth song), Brahms adored what was loosely called 'Hungarian' music. We should remember in this respect that it was Schubert, not Liszt, who pioneered the art of the Hungarian rhapsody, and that Liszt did not see its possibilities until he arranged for solo piano a portion of Schubert's four-handed *Hungarian Divertissement*.

In the *Liebeslieder* waltzes, Brahms had Georg Friedrich Daumer's translations of Eastern European folk poems to serve as a *raison d'être* for his mixing of Hungarian and Viennese idioms in these scintillating waltzes, which he marked to be played 'Im Ländler-Tempo' in tribute to their Schubertian origins. In so doing, he resourcefully employed the voices in a variety of ways, sometimes in chorus, sometimes in duet and sometimes very charmingly in solo capacity.

Among recordings of the Op. 54 *Liebeslieder*, Benjamin Britten's, with the galaxy of performers listed above, catches the mingled flavours of the music to a nicety. Fears that the effect might sound too arch and English, particularly with Peter Pears as tenor, are quickly dispatched. This is the most congenial of concert parties, eked out with enchanting odds and ends by Rossini and Tchaikovsky (BBC Music Legends BBCB8001-2).

Those who would have preferred the extra space on the disc to be devoted to the *Neueliebeslieder*, Op. 65, can obtain both sets of songs in equally engaging performances by Edith Mathis, Brigitte Fassbaender, Peter Schreier and Dietrich Fischer-Dieskau, with Karl Engel and Wolfgang Sawallisch as pianists (DG 423 133-2). The more authentically German line-up of voices here brings greater authority to the singing without the slightest loss of charm. Happy should be the record-collector who possesses either of these performances.

The Brahms who inscribed a copy of *The Blue Danube* with the words 'Unfortunately not by Johannes Brahms' did not confine his flair for light music to love songs. As someone who adored playing Hungarian gypsy music on the piano, he adapted twenty-one such pieces to his own style, arranged them captivatingly for piano duet in the same year as he composed his first book of *Liebeslieder* waltzes, and entitled them *Hungarian Dances* while admitting that the tunes were not his own.

As with Liszt's Hungarian Rhapsodies, these dances were not the outcome of meticulous forensic research into the roots of Hungarian folk music in the future manner of Bartók or Kodály. Brahms took the music as he found it, arranged it with gusto and Brahmsified it so thoroughly that people assumed it to be all his own work. No. 1, in this respect, is a favourite encore piece, especially in Brahms's own orchestral arrangement. The witty No. 3 and the racy, rumbustious No. 10 also exist in Brahms orchestrations.

All the established orchestral versions, including some by the Brahms authority Hans Gal, can thus be described as arrangements of arrangements, which does not lessen their attractiveness. But if this, in terms of purism, makes them a bit of a minefield for musicologists, it should be remembered that they were not a minefield to Brahms, who loved them and regarded them simply as part of the Viennese scene, to be enjoyed by the same people who swayed to the strains of Strauss waltzes.

Recordings of Brahms's *Hungarian Dances* are even more of a minefield than the pieces themselves. Some of them simply miss the style of the music, some are too brash, some irritatingly over-sophisticated, and Ivan Fischer's with his Budapest Festival Orchestra thoroughly de-Brahmsifies them with the addition of genuine gypsy violins and a genuine Hungarian cimbalom. For all Fischer's good intentions, authenticity of this sort sounds like falsehood. Bogar and the Budapest Symphony Orchestra are much to be preferred in performances which not only are spontaneous and as true as it is possible to be to Brahms but also come at bargain-basement price (Naxos 8.550110).

In the end, however, it is in Brahms's own four-handed piano versions that the dances really sparkle, as a recording by Silke-Thora Matthies and Christian Kohn conclusively demonstrates. With the composer's own piano duet arrangements of the first set of *Liebeslieder* waltzes as coupling, this is clearly the disc to buy (Naxos 8.553140).

Eight

1873
STRING QUARTET NO. 1 IN C MINOR,
OP. 51, NO. 1

Allegro   Romanze: Poco adagio

Allegretto molto moderato e comodo; un poco piu animato   Allegro

Brahms, a master of chamber music, destroyed all but three of his string quartets because they failed to meet his exacting standards. Whether he was neurotically self-critical to have put so much music – reputedly as many as twenty works – to the torch is something we shall never know, because he prudently left no sketches for posterity to pore over and attempt to perform.

Even when, at the mature age of 40, he cautiously released the two quartets that form his Op. 51, he noted gloomily that he was doing so 'for the second time'. By this he meant that he had already insisted on hearing them played secretly by the Florentine Quartet and been dissatisfied with them. Not until they had been substantially revised and given a further test run by a different ensemble did he declare the music to be 'perhaps' almost ready for performance.

So we can count ourselves lucky that, after more changes, the C minor Quartet, Op. 51, No. 1, and its A minor companion piece, were ultimately allowed to see the light of day. Not that either of them could be called a day-lit work. The C minor Quartet, like the C minor symphony (No. 1) of the same period, had gone through a prolonged and painful gestation, audible (even if to say so may seem wise after the event) in every note of the music. As far back as 1865, Brahms had informed the violinist and quartet leader, Joseph Joachim, that he had started to write a work in that key, though whether it was the same work as the one he eventually produced eight years later was never divulged.

When feeling his way into what for him was a new area of composition, Brahms was invariably assailed by doubts. But though the laborious effort required by the C minor Quartet speaks through the music, only the most fanatical anti-Brahmsian could call it a laboured work. Heavyweight symphonic tension was a natural aspect of Brahms's musical personality. Rich textures were a feature even of his chamber music. A dependence on double-stopped string tone was therefore, as the Edinburgh-based musical analyst, Sir Donald Tovey, once put it, only to be expected from the fullness of harmony necessary for even the most ascetic statement of Brahms's ideas.

The opening *allegro* moves and heaves, flares up and dies down, with a stormy determination which, whether you like it or not, is powerfully impressive. People have spoken of its 'fevered rhetoric', its 'strenuous energy' and its 'dark passion', followed in the slow movement with viola tone sounding like 'a pair of deep-sea horns'. For Schoenberg, who was no half-hearted admirer of Brahms, the harmonic richness of the music was comparable with Wagner's *Tristan*.

Brahms himself, being a devotee of Beethoven, was thought to have chosen C minor as the key of his first published string quartet because it harked back to the 'fateful' C minor of Beethoven's Fifth Symphony. But if that was the case, his refusal to allow the music to reach triumphant C major in the finale took fatefulness a stage further than Beethoven went and, indeed, further than Brahms himself would go in his own C minor symphony, with its C major conclusion, which he completed soon after the final release of the quartet.

The quartet, indeed, has a relentless circling quality that provides no scope for 'happy' endings, nor for any diversion from its main argument, which is powerfully sustained from first note to last. Nothing is permitted to lighten its tone. The *Romanze* which forms the slow movement must therefore be taken with a pinch of salt. If the music is songlike, it is songlike in the most regretfully Brahmsian sense. If it is glowing, it is a glow in the dark. The third movement maintains the mood. Neither a scherzo nor even one of Brahms's lyrical intermezzos, it is a grey, impassive bridge between whatever small comforts have been provided by the slow movement and their total withdrawal in the agitated finale. In spite of occasional hints of a possible C major outcome, the music is brought back inexorably to its C minor starting point.

In attempting to convey what has been perceptively called the Faustian struggle of this work, many ensembles merely sound turgid – which is why, for years, Brahms was considered no great shakes as a composer of string quartets. Yet the truth lies in the music, not those performances which, through no fault of the composer, end up sounding constipated.

As a distinguished, highly sophisticated Viennese exponent of this work, the Alban Berg Quartet has been hailed as the one which knows how to get it right. Its EMI recording certainly combines passion with sensitivity, colour with attack. Dating from 1991, it forms part of a two-disc set of Brahms's three surviving works in the form (754829-2); but a more recent performance by the young, British-based Belcea Quartet – whose members happen to be protégés of the Alban Bergs – has the edge in terms of tonal beauty and keen rhythmic vitality. Brahms's G major String Quintet is here the splendid coupling, with Thomas Kakuska (from the senior quartet) as the extra viola player in a wonderfully fresh-toned performance (EMI 5 57661 2).

Nine

1876
SYMPHONY NO. 1 IN C MINOR, OP. 68

Un poco sostenuto – Allegro   Andante sostenuto

Un poco allegretto e grazioso

Adagio – Piu andante – Allegro ma non troppo, ma con brio

'Long and not exactly amiable' was Brahms's typically gruff description
of his First Symphony, completed at the age of 43, fourteen years after he
had sent a sketch of its first movement to his friend Clara Schumann. She
reported herself surprised to receive it, but commented that she enjoyed
it 'in great drafts'. Brahms, a neurotically uncertain symphonist, had
already transformed a previous such work into his first piano concerto.
Then he had produced his *Alto Rhapsody*, his *Variations on a Theme of
Haydn*, and much fine chamber music in further avoidance of the issue.
Yet his would-be Symphony No. 1 would not go away. By the time he

completed it, the teenage Mahler and Richard Strauss were heading for fame, and Beethoven (with whom he had long feared comparison) had been dead for half a century. Brahms was running late, but at least he was conscious of the fact, and he triumphed in the end. His symphony in C minor – Beethoven's favourite key of conflict – rose above the gibes that musicians of the period hurled at it.

The Beethovenian overtones, as Brahms himself asserted, were in any case irrelevant. The first movement's portentous and certainly not exactly amiable introduction is wholly Brahmsian in tension and texture, with the wind and strings straining against each other, while the kettledrums maintain a menacing beat. Out of these opening pages the entire movement evolves. In the main *allegro* section, signposted by a loud, sudden drum thwack, the conflict intensifies. Though the woodwind and horns provide moments of uneasy calm, the music is mostly sinewy and restless, its pulse increasingly like that of some grimly grinding scherzo which, when it finally reaches its abrasive climax, stops suddenly in its tracks. Thereafter, the energy subsides and a back-reference to the slow introduction, with a brief glimpse of the work's C major goal, brings the movement to its close.

But C major is still a long way off. The slow movement, which Eduard Hanslick – Vienna's pro-Brahmsian, anti-Wagnerian critic – described as 'a sustained, noble song', turns instead to the unexpectedly distant key of E major. This was a choice Beethoven had also made for the slow movement of his C minor Piano Concerto, and it bestows a similarly soft glow upon the music. From the strings, shaded by bassoon tone, comes a tender, lyrical melody, and from the oboe an even more tender extension of it. Another oboe melody, moving more nimbly, generates activity in the rest of the orchestra before the opening mood is restored. The first of the oboe melodies is repeated in new and poetic colours by horn and solo violin, a radiant masterstroke by a composer sometimes dismissed as a severely functional orchestrator.

Sustaining the mood, the third movement is a clarinet intermezzo of a very Brahmsian sort. It postpones the forthcoming struggle between C minor and C major by being cast in the key of A flat major, and is characterised by the leisurely and very definitely amiable melody with which it opens. In the trio section, a sturdy, swinging theme erupts in the minor and spreads through the orchestra before the clarinet melody returns with some simple but beautiful embellishments.

The finale, by far the biggest of the four movements, brings the music back to its C minor roots before battling its way to C major. Muttering pizzicato passages and fierce swirls of string tone set the stage for drama. Then, with a powerful, rather Wagnerian drum roll, the atmosphere suddenly clears and the horns sound a golden bell-like theme (known in Britain as the 'Cambridge chimes' but in fact inspired by an old alphorn tune Brahms had once jotted on a birthday card to Clara Schumann) over shimmering strings.

The trombones then harmonise a solemn chorale, and the *allegro* section is launched with the broad melody which, to Brahms's discomfort, Hanslick compared with the *Ode to Joy* from Beethoven's Ninth Symphony. But Brahms was right to feel irritated. The melody is thoroughly Brahmsian and has its own Brahmsian integrity. Moreover, since it has already been heard, in a disguised and gloomy C minor version at the start of the finale, its grandly sonorous and thoroughly organic emergence as the main theme of the *allegro* sounds all the more impressive. At the close of the movement, the trombone theme is brought back — louder, faster and more jubilant, if the conductor does it the way Brahms intended — to deliver the symphony inexorably into a blaze of sunlight.

Being the biggest and grandest of Brahms's four symphonies, the first tends to be treated to the biggest and grandest performances by conductors — Karajan, Bernstein and so on — who see it largely as their own ego trip. With violins massed to the left of them, up to ten double basses to the right, and double-strength woodwind in the middle, the music emerges as Brahms soup, and audiences have grown so accustomed to having it served in this manner that anything lighter-weight makes them feel cheated.

But less, in Brahmsian terms, is almost invariably more. Brahms composed for orchestras of fifty or fewer players, and himself preferred to conduct orchestras of that size, in which string tone was never obese, rhythms were sharpened by hard-headed drumsticks, and the woodwind could be heard with ease. That is the sort of sound Sir Charles Mackerras and the Scottish Chamber Orchestra supply in their recording of the four symphonies 'in the style of the original Meiningen performances', and the result is revelatory.

The lean, lithe account of the First Symphony strips the music of the dull bottom-heaviness from which it usually suffers. To suggest that Brahms, if only he had been able to hear it, would have preferred the sound of a big modern orchestra in a plush modern concert hall simply sidesteps the issue. Such a performance is an entirely different, infinitely less Brahmsian experience, and we need conductors like Mackerras to remind us of the fact. His three-disc set of the four symphonies, with some shorter works as fillers, is required listening not only for anyone who wants to know more about Brahms, but also – which is what matters in the end – because it is an enthralling, exhilarating experience (Telarc CD-80450).

For a performance less historically informed, yet true to Brahms, Gunter Wand's with the North German Radio Orchestra reaches to the heart of the music without imposing too much of the conductor's own personality upon it. The inclusion – and on a single disc – of the Symphony No. 3 makes this an attractive issue (RCA 74321 68009-2). It is, however, inevitably surpassed by Otto Klemperer's vintage recording with the Philharmonia Orchestra, dating from the 1950s but still possessing a sense of structure and rhythm that make it seem written in stone. With the *Tragic Overture* and the *Alto Rhapsody* (sung by Christa Ludwig) as fillers, this is one of the Brahms discs of all time (EMI 5 67029-2).

Ten

1877
SYMPHONY NO. 2 IN D MAJOR, OP. 73

Allegro non troppo

Adagio non troppo

Allegretto grazioso

Allegro con spirito

Sir Thomas Beecham, that wittiest of programme planners, liked to preface his performances of Brahms's Symphony No. 2 in D with Beethoven's Symphony No. 2 in the same key, after he had conducted a short curtain-raiser in the form of Clementi's Symphony No. 2, also in D. It meant a lot of one single key in one single concert; but D major, coming from Beecham, was synonymous with musical sunshine rather than boredom. Not for nothing did he select Brahms's symphony as the natural extension of Beethoven's in terms of lyricism, energy and humour. Nor for nothing, being the conductor he was, did he prize Brahms's Second Symphony above the same composer's three other, more portentous, works in symphonic form.

Though Brahms saw himself as a summer composer, who spent the rest of the year revising, perfecting, proof-reading and conducting what he had written on his holidays from Vienna, not much of his music sounds quite as summery as this. Inspired, like his Violin Concerto (also in D), by the beauty of Lake Wörth in southern Austria – Alban Berg, some sixty years later, would compose his Violin Concerto on the opposite shore of the same lake – the Second Symphony has a luminosity of texture, a melodic serenity and a rhythmic impulse of a very special sort, which Brahms would never again achieve to quite such idyllic effect. To call it carefree might seem to be stretching a point, or claiming too much of a composer characterised more frequently by musical stresses and strains. But it is a masterpiece as light-hearted as Brahms ever produced, and its closing pages, in a good performance, possess a jubilation almost unique in his output.

The swiftness with which he completed this work in 1877 – a mere year after the mighty labour pains of the Symphony No. 1 – speaks for itself. Of that long and powerful minor-key symphony, it is the calmer and more succinct major-key obverse. Yet, in its first two movements, it does not lack spaciousness. The unhurried opening notes – a swaying phrase for cellos and basses, a sweet shimmer of horn tone – suggest the scope of the music to follow, almost all of which turns out to be influenced in one way or another by these fragmentary ideas. A soft but not ominous roll on the kettledrums and a melody airily floated by the violins sustain the impression of a symphony at ease with itself, which will take no short-cuts to its destination. True, one optional short-cut — the omission of the first movement's big exposition repeat — is traditionally regarded as perfectly acceptable, perhaps even desirable, though Brahms himself invariably took care to conduct the movement in full, in which case it lasts at least twenty minutes.

Yet, in spite of its general tranquillity, the first movement does have a growing intensity of expression and a very real central point of climax where the opening horn call is dissonantly ground out by the trombones, which are sparingly employed in this work but always to great effect. The intensity, however, is mostly held in check by the movement's prevailing waltz-like pulse; and the coda, when it arrives, is filled with teasing understatements, including some whimsical — and certainly unexpected — harbingers of neo-classical Stravinsky in the woodwind.

Brahmsian sunshine being dependent on Brahmsian shadow, the *adagio* begins darkly with the sound of cello and bassoon tone in stark counterpoint, the instruments unblended and proceeding in contrary motion. The key is now B major, but it sounds almost like B minor, the effect suggestive perhaps of a solitary walk in a dense forest, with sunlight gleaming through the trees. Again there is a gradual intensification of expression, and again a distinct, indeed quite passionate, point of climax before a sense of slightly melancholy peacefulness is retrieved.

But if the *adagio* has its sombre side, the third movement — a superb example of the sort of semi-scherzo which was Brahms's answer to

Beethoven – is amiably bucolic. Set in motion by a dancelike oboe tune with a charming flick on its third beat, it incorporates two faster-paced trio sections in which offbeat accents are again a feature. The ending is faintly wistful, and the quietly monochrome start of the finale gives little hint of the merriment to follow. But it makes the blaze of colour, when it suddenly bursts forth, seem all the more resplendent. There is an opulent second subject, rich in string tone, which causes the music to lose impetus if, as too often happens, the conductor too conspicuously slackens speed at this point.

Later there comes a moment of special magic when the movement's hazily soft introductory material reappears in a mysterious middle section. But the recapitulation soon sweeps aside these developments with unswerving vivacity. The trombones return, the banners unfurl and the glowing second subject brings this adorable symphony to its euphoric close.

Sir Charles Mackerras and the Scottish Chamber Orchestra are again just the right performers for this work, because their touch is light and fleet, the textures never coagulate and the valveless horns which the conductor gifted to this orchestra are heard to marvellous effect, especially in the first movement. As part of a comprehensive symphonic set, upon which Mackerras imposes a vigorously stylish overview, this is the performance to go for (Telarc CD-800450).

In comparison, Otto Klemperer's famous recording with the Philhar-monia Orchestra seems a little intimidating, though his account of the

Third Symphony, with which it is coupled, benefits from his severity of approach (EMI 5 67030-2). It is Sir Thomas Beecham, however, who brings out the real radiance of the music in a live 1956 Edinburgh Festival performance with the Royal Philharmonic which has gone down in history.

The dreary first half of the concert had featured Sir Arthur Bliss as conductor of his own *Edinburgh* overture and Violin Concerto. Beecham, arriving too early for his own portion of the programme, had amused himself backstage by tossing the clothes of the Master of the Queen's Music out of the green room and into the corridor of the Usher Hall. Then, ready for further mischief, he mounted to platform level while Bliss was conducting and distracted the players by gesticulating at them through the glass door leading to the stage. The Brahms which followed after the interval was naturally electrifying and, as the BBC recording (for all its imperfections) reveals, prompted the audience to burst wildly into applause before the last chord had stopped sounding (BBCL 4099-2).

Eleven

1878
VIOLIN CONCERTO IN D MAJOR, OP. 77

Allegro non troppo   Adagio

Allegro giocoso, ma non troppo vivace

At the time of its premiere, Brahms's Violin Concerto was dismissed by Hans von Bülow, the finest conductor in Europe, as a concerto 'against' the violin. It was a harsh response to a warm-hearted, beautifully written, symphonically coherent, deeply violinistic and indeed rapturous work. Yet he was not alone in his judgement of it. The Polish virtuoso Henryk Wieniawski, to whom Brahms had shown the manuscript, declared it unplayable, and his Spanish rival Pablo de Sarasate made the same point rather differently when asked if he intended to learn the new concerto. 'Do you think', he replied, 'I could stoop so low as to listen, violin in hand, to the oboe playing the only proper tune in the entire work?'

Tunes, it's true, sometimes fail to be recognised instantly for what they are – how else could Verdi's *Rigoletto* once have been deemed unmelodic?

What Sarasate was unable to perceive, apart from missing all the tunes in the vast sweep of the first movement and in the gypsy vitality of the finale, was that the melody which the oboe plays at the start of the slow movement, lovely though it is, sounds even lovelier when the violinist decoratively meditates upon it soon afterwards. In other words, Brahms knew exactly what he was doing in giving it to the oboe in the first place. Fritz Kreisler, at least, recognised this when he reported that the happiest of all his musical experiences were the times he played Brahms's *adagio* in London with the oboist Leon Goossens.

It was, in any case, far from being the concerto's only inspiring point of melodic interest. When he composed it, in the summer of 1878, Brahms was sojourning at Portschach, the Austrian lakeside resort where he had written his sunlit Second Symphony the previous year. It was a place, he asserted, where melodies flew about so abundantly you had to be careful not to step on them. The two works, indeed, have much in common, not just because they are in the same bright major key, but because they employ arpeggio formations as the basis of important themes, not least (in each case) the main theme of the first movement.

Since Brahms himself — like Beethoven before him — was primarily a pianist, he valued the advice he received from the concerto's original soloist and dedicatee, his friend Joseph Joachim, about various technical aspects of the music. Yet the long-established anecdote that the writing of this work resolved a deep and lengthy rift between the two men is quite untrue. It was in 1880, two years later, that they fell out with each other, after Brahms had sided tactlessly with Joachim's wife Amalie during a marital dispute which ended in divorce. The work which finally healed the wound was the drabber and less familiar Double Concerto for violin and cello, not written until 1887.

Meanwhile, back in 1878, Brahms was grateful that Joachim – himself an able composer – was willing to provide his own substantial cadenza for the Violin Concerto, which soon established itself as an essential part of the first movement (though there are other cadenzas also worth playing). Whether Brahms was so grateful when, at the work's second performance, the audience applauded the cadenza 'right into my coda' – the implication being that one of the most serenely lovely passages in the entire concerto was thereby rendered inaudible – was something he diplomatically failed to dwell upon. What he certainly objected to was Joachim's desire to perform Beethoven's Violin Concerto in the same programme ('too much D major'); but it was Joachim who won his way.

The premiere itself, on the other hand, seemed to satisfy Joachim the soloist as much as it satisfied Brahms the conductor, even if the performance made no great impression on the original audience. Joachim's own reservations about the work had been slight. 'Much of it is really original and violinistic', he said of the first movement, while adding warily that he could not say definitely that it would play comfortably in a hot concert room until he had the music at his fingertips.

At this stage in the work's genesis, however, the music was still in a far from final state, with four movements instead of what ultimately became three. Brahms, brooding about its layout, characteristically jettisoned the two central movements as 'failures' (one of them eventually became the superb scherzo of the Second Piano Concerto), and in their place he provided what he (again typically) referred to as a 'feeble' *adagio*. Such radical restructuring delayed the first performance, which Joachim had hoped to give in Berlin in December 1878, until 1 January in Leipzig, where every year, by a happy custom, the great violinist appeared as soloist in the Gewandhaus on New Year's Day.

Yet Hans von Bülow's sarcastic criticism of the concerto was not wholly wrong. Though by no means written 'against' the violin – something a soloist as vain as Joachim would hardly have found acceptable – it was a work in which the orchestra played an uncommonly important role. The violin part, for all its difficulty, was not intended as a display of virtuosity but was closely integrated with what, in concerto parlance, continues to be called the 'accompaniment'.

In some respects, this seemed to the soloist's disadvantage, though not to that of the work itself, which, like Berlioz's *Harold in Italy*, benefited from the presence of a soloist who was almost part of the orchestra. Brahms's, in fact, was not only a violin concerto, one of the greatest of its kind, but also a concerto 'with' violin or, as one commentator has perceptively put it, a 'symphonic lyric' incorporating a solo violin.

In other respects, however, it is a thoroughly classical concerto, beginning with a large-scale orchestral statement of the main themes of the first movement before the entry of the soloist. This was something which composers like Mendelssohn and Max Bruch (and Beethoven before them in two of his piano concertos) had done away with, by bringing the soloist into the action immediately. Yet, in Brahms's Violin Concerto, the belated entry of the soloist, playing the main theme in a minor key, is undoubtedly one of the work's masterstrokes, as is the violin's subsequent introduction of a nervy new melody with triple-stops.

As for the coda, sabotaged during the work's second performance by applause for Joachim's cadenza, the serenity of the last soft airborne transfiguration of the main theme by the soloist is one of the work's most magical moments, preparing the way for the similarly tranquil opening of the 'feeble' *adagio*. The poetic seriousness of the first two movements, however, is ultimately replaced by the jocular exuberance of a finale in the manner of Brahms's Hungarian dances.

Again the interplay between soloist and orchestra is of major importance, though Joachim (who was responsible for adding the marking *ma non troppo vivace* to Brahms's *Allegro giocoso*) was right to advise a degree of restraint if the exhilarating energy of the coda was to make its effect when the performers finally reached it.

Since there are few violinists today who have failed to show their prowess in Brahms's Violin Concerto, there is naturally no shortage of recordings of this much-loved work. Among the old masters, Jascha Heifetz in his fifties gave an exhilaratingly virile, vividly articulated account of it, shunning the soulfulness of Yehudi Menuhin in this music and challenging Fritz Reiner and the Chicago Symphony Orchestra to keep up with him. The disc includes Tchaikovsky's Violin Concerto for good measure (RCA 09026 61495-2).

Perhaps the only modern interpreter who can match him is Gidon Kremer, who likewise shuns soulfulness along with the hitherto obligatory Joachim cadenza, here replaced by an enthrallingly Brahmsian rhapsody by George Enescu. The presence of Nikolaus Harnoncourt as conductor ensures that the orchestra, the Royal Concertgebouw, rises far above accompanimental level, and the inclusion of the Double Concerto, in which Kremer is joined by Clemens Hagen in a crackling performance, is generous to say the least (Teldec 0630-13137-2).

If Kremer has a living rival, it is Maxim Vengerov, whose performance with Daniel Barenboim and the Chicago Symphony Orchestra sounds sensationally spontaneous, admittedly at the expense of the work's dreamier moments. Again there is a novel cadenza, this time by the soloist himself. The coupling is Brahms's Third Violin Sonata, performed by Vengerov and Barenboim (Teldec 0630-17144-2).

Twelve

1879
SONATA NO. 1 IN G MAJOR FOR VIOLIN AND PIANO, OP. 78

Vivace ma non troppo   Adagio   Allegro molto moderato

Brahms was a master of the opening paragraph. It was a quality, obviously, which he shared with other composers, but which calls for immediate mention in the case of his G major Violin Sonata and its two successors. Not all violin sonatas can be said to start effectively. The tonal clash between the two instruments and the inevitable question of balance are things which some composers, and some players, handle better than others.

But the point about this sonata is that it begins so sweetly, so beautifully, so invitingly that you are instantly won over to what it has to say. It is not just the melodic flow, not just the subtle spacing of the piano chords, not just the way the instruments, gradually but intentionally, seem at one point to go out of phase with each other. This happens not far from the start, when one of them is playing two beats in the bar, the other in three-time, yet never so as to give the impression that something is going seriously wrong.

It is a familiar Brahmsian device, nowhere more deftly employed than here. His supreme ability to float the music, to keep us guessing about it and steadily to intensify it, is what draws us into the first movement and prepares us for the arrival of the next important theme, no less attractive than the first, but more boldly voiced in clear-cut three-time. The whole movement, indeed, has an increasing passion and vitality, in which the piano's role is never less interesting than the violin's — indeed, one of the most magical moments comes when the piano plays the opening theme against soft pizzicato notes from the violin.

The *adagio* promises more of the same, opening as it does with another very beautiful theme, full of Brahmsian warmth and first played with rich E flat major resonance by the piano. But then, with the entry of the violin, something happens. The music starts to sigh, and the violin's takeover of the theme does nothing to lift this air of sadness. The piano, with tolling, thudding rhythms, sounds darkly funereal, and the violin adds its voice to the mood of mourning. In one of his letters to Clara Schumann around this time, Brahms said that she and her chronically tubercular son Felix formed the inspiration of this movement. The ending, like the beginning, is very lovely, but the cloudless sky of the opening movement does not return.

Brahms, famously a summer composer, wrote this first of his violin sonatas at Pörtschach on the Wörthersee, one of his favourite resorts. It was where he had already produced his Violin Concerto and the second (and warmest) of his symphonies. But these dated from 1877 and 1878, and this was 1879. Was it the weather or simply his mood which prompted him to base the finale on the 'rain' songs he had once written to poems by his friend Klaus Groth?

The idea of selecting a song as inspiration for one of the movements of a large-scale work had previously been employed by Schubert in his 'Trout' quintet and Violin Fantasy. The words which inspired Brahms tell of how the patter of raindrops brings memories of childhood and makes you 'mourn the young days dead and gone' – a very Brahmsian sort of sentiment. It is perhaps this remembrance of old forgotten far-off things which gives not only the finale but also the previous movements of the sonata, where there are many hints of the rain music before its ultimate identifiable emergence, a special melancholy beauty.

The piano, at any rate, maintains a softly running, indeed quite rainy, accompaniment to the violin's melodic line. The music shows leanings towards the minor, and the effect throughout seems troubled and wintry, not at all serene. Flashbacks to the theme of the *adagio* fail to cheer things up – indeed, they do rather the reverse – but in the closing bars a hint of the first movement's original sweetness is touchingly regained. When Brahms sent a copy of this sonata to Clara Schumann, by then in her seventies, she replied that she hoped the music would accompany her on her journey into the next world.

To claim that Brahms's First Violin Sonata is in some way more special than its two successors, written almost ten years later, perhaps says more about oneself than about Brahms. All three works are superb, of course; and, when presented within a single recital, as they quite often are, they form a triptych of richly expressive self-portraits. The Second Sonata, Op. 100 in A major, dating from 1886, is sunnier – indeed, one of Brahms's last genuinely sunny works – and the Third, Op. 108 in D minor, completed in 1888, is concentrated, declamatory, very passionate and direct, for many people the finest of the three.

A recording containing the entire triptych, rather than just the G major Sonata, is thus the right thing to acquire, since the music forms such a unity of contrasts and fits neatly on to a single disc. Christian Tetzlaff and Lars Vogt, a fine young German duo, have obliged with a performance recorded live at the 2002 Heimbach Chamber Music Festival, fortunately without the sort of audience intrusion described with such dark comedy by Julian Barnes in one of his collections of short stories, *The Lemon Table*.

An obsolete German power station may seem an improbable setting for Brahms, but these works have their own German power, and the sound is admirable. Brahms's pounding scherzo from the *FAE* ('Free but Lonely') *Sonata*, a composite work to which Schumann and Albert Dietrich also contributed, forms a thoroughly apt encore (EMI Classics 5 57525 2).

Augustin Dumay and Maria João Pires, whose recording of the Beethoven violin sonatas shows such closeness of feeling for the music, bring similar finesse to the three Brahms sonatas (DG 435 800-2). But they are matched, even outmatched, by Krysia Osostowicz and Susan Tomes in performances where musical conversation matters more than declamation (Hyperion Helios CDH 55087).

Thirteen

1881
PIANO CONCERTO NO. 2 IN B FLAT MAJOR, OP. 83

Allegro non troppo

Andante

Allegro appassionato

Allegretto grazioso

Brahms's two piano concertos are essentially symphonic conceptions rather than virtuoso display pieces or battles between soloist and orchestra. Nevertheless, they remain among the most challenging, strenuous, big-toned works in the repertoire, requiring a pianist with stamina as well as brainpower. Both works cost their composer immense effort. The first of them, in D minor, was his first major work on a grand scale, and went through considerable metamorphosis before achieving its perfected form in 1858. The second was begun twenty years later, and took three years to complete.

Though Brahms regarded himself as a summer composer, responding to the instant inspiration of lakeside holidays in Switzerland and Austria, the piano concertos do not sound like instant works. Each was weightily premeditated, and the second started life as an offshoot of his Violin Concerto, which he had composed at some speed in 1878. Having intended, innovatively, to incorporate a scherzo as one of its movements, he encountered such opposition from his violinist, Joseph Joachim, that he abandoned the idea. His sketches for it, however, formed the basis of his new piano concerto's similarly unconventional second movement, which, with Brahms himself as soloist, received no opposition at all.

Aware of the work's resultant marathon scale — not until Busoni composed his Piano Concerto would there be a masterpiece so massive — Brahms characteristically made light of it by saying he had composed a 'tiny, tiny piano concerto with a tiny, tiny wisp of a scherzo'. On hearing this news, his pianist friend Clara Schumann responded: 'I don't at all believe it's as small as you pretend, though I shall be pleased if it is, because I might then be capable of playing it.' Her fears were those of other female pianists. For long it was considered 'not a woman's piece', though that restriction has now been lifted.

Brahms himself forecast that his second concerto would sound very different from the first. His prophecy was accurate. Time, after all, had passed. His very appearance had changed, via the acquisition of a beard and a belly — 'clean-shaven', he explained, 'people take you for an actor or a priest'. The piano part, for all its weight, is sprightlier and (apart for the thundery scherzo) sunnier than that of the earlier concerto. The finale, after the richness of the preceding movements, has astonishing lightness of touch. Trumpets and drums drop out of the picture. The music glides and gushes serenely to its close.

But the start of the concerto, despite its idyllic horn call, is rather different. The piano's entry, requiring a compass of more than five octaves, develops into a quasi-cadenza whose assertiveness is surpassed only by a later re-entry signalled by three massive chords. This is no 'tiny, tiny' concerto but one in which the thematic figures of this expository section suggest how varied and intricate the movement is going to be. The gentle poetry of the opening horn call changes into music more martial. Sweetness becomes sadness. The piano engages in transformations of the main themes, sometimes with delicacy, sometimes with huge handfuls of trills and double octaves. The coda – one of Brahms's great moments of inspiration – climbs out of prolonged darkness into sudden radiance.

The mellowness of the work's substantial slow movement, however, is not yet imminent. Having achieved the full security of B flat major at the end of the first movement, Brahms immediately undermines it with his smoky scherzo in D minor, where the hard-won serenity of his new concerto is invaded by a grim memory of its predecessor. The music glowers and hurtles, gets rid of its tensions in the swinging major-key central section, then lurches back into sombre ferocity.

The calm resumption of B flat major in the slow movement shows why the scherzo was so essential to Brahms's overall scheme. A solo cello sings an exquisite, though treacherous, song without words, which Brahms would later transform into a true song, the lovely *Immer leiser wird mein Schlummer* ('My sleep grows ever quieter'). An English critic who, in *The Observer*, once dismissed this meandering theme as 'detumescent' was promptly challenged by the conductor Sir Malcolm Sargent who, in a letter to the editor, deemed it nothing of the kind. Impotent or otherwise, the long cello solo fails to steal the piano's limelight. With horn and clarinet as other voices, the movement proceeds in the manner of Brahms's choicest, most beautifully integrated chamber music, exploring the distant key of F sharp major before ultimately finding its way back to the opening cello melody, with piano embellishments.

From here, the B flat major gaiety of the finale is easily reached. But, although seriousness is firmly suppressed, it is not at the expense of quality control. The succession of themes in Brahms's Hungarian mode, each captivatingly unfurled by the pianist and whirling away, it has been said, in a glory of tumbling gaiety, is a marvellous demonstration of keyboard finesse. The wit speaks for itself, and the fact that it is Brahmsian does not make it any the less polished or perfectly timed.

Though Alfred Brendel has spoken of Brahms's 'unsurpassable pianistic perversions' in this work, and has given up performing it himself, its challenges have been relished by pianists such as Sir Clifford Curzon, who might have been expected to back away from them. Maurizio Pollini, in his magisterial recording with Claudio Abbado and the Berlin Philharmonic, certainly does not do that. Never can the music have seemed more profoundly mastered, more powerfully delivered – and this in a live performance with all the work's nerve-ends mercilessly exposed.

In a London performance in the 1960s, Rudolf Serkin once brought his hands down startlingly early on the greatest chord in the first movement; but Pollini makes no such blunders. His *sang-froid* never deserts him yet never casts an atmosphere of chill over this magnificently warm-hearted score (DG 453 505-2).

Fourteen

1882
PIANO TRIO IN C MAJOR, OP. 87

Allegro

Andante con moto

Scherzo: Presto

Finale: Allegro giocoso

In its two hugely contrasted versions, Brahms's big B major Piano Trio, Op. 8, chronologically straddles this somewhat shorter but no less impressive work in C major. First composed in 1854, the B major Trio was so substantially revised in 1889 that it gained almost a whole new physiognomy in the process. Both versions remain valid, though the 1889 is the more coherent and the more frequently performed. With the C major Trio, however, there are no such options. The ever-disgruntled composer was sufficiently happy with it to produce only one version, though two whole years separate the composition of the first movement in the summer of 1880 from that of the rest of the work in the summer of 1882.

But Brahms was never famed for speed. Obsessively self-critical, he was always ready to rewrite a work, completely change its format, delay its publication or, if he felt so inclined, destroy it. Neither the B major trio (in whichever version) nor the C major, fortunately, seems to have been at serious risk. But, if his belief in them required outside support, it lay close to hand in the person, as so often, of Clara Schumann. Not only did he love her with his own quietly Brahmsian discretion, but he also relied on her opinion as a friend and musician.

So when he sent the completed manuscript of Op. 87 to her for comment, he must have been relieved to receive the following reply: 'A trio like yours was a real musical tonic – how I would love to hear it properly played. I love every moment and how wonderfully it is developed. I am so charmed with the way in which one motif grows out of another.' Musical development being one of Brahms's specialities, and the C major Trio being conspicuously strong in that area, her words must have come as no real surprise to him. To her diary, however, she confided some observations more severe: 'I am not', she wrote, 'really satisfied with it as a whole, except for the *andante*. It is a pity he does not always polish his work or cut out dull passages.' Had she communicated her true thoughts to the composer, we might not have had an Op. 87 to listen to today.

Happily, his confidence remained undamaged (though he took pains to destroy the first movement of another trio, in E flat major, which he had begun alongside the C major). Indeed, the music shows a fresh command of all three instruments. Having given the piano the lion's share of the B major Trio, he found new ways of enabling the violin and cello to compete with it on more positive terms.

Here, it is upon the strings that he bestows the opening theme of the first movement, demoting the piano to an accompanying role. Even if it soon regains some of its old dominance in the unfurling of transition passages and in the array of themes which combine to form the second subject, the strings are still given plenty to do — not least when the music swirls to its close with the main theme transformed into something approaching the sound of a Viennese waltz.

The minor-key slow movement is a very Brahmsian inspiration, a theme and five variations in melancholy Hungarian gypsy vein, with a trudging beat and a few gentle rays of sunshine when the music moves briefly into the major. Crisp breezes dart and ripple through the succeeding scherzo, a brilliant study in Brahmsian minimalism but surely also an impressionistic waterscape of the rivers and lakes around Bad Ischl, the Austrian spa where he composed it.

As has been suggested more than once, the movement portrays a twilight world, full of lights and half-lights, with fleeting shadows and half-perceived shapes between the trees. The piano part, as one pianist has noted, requires lightning reflexes. The music briefly burgeons into a glowing, swaying middle section in the major (which Clara Schumann for some reason found 'not imposing enough') before the cool breezes resume.

The finale counterbalances the first movement with a wealth of themes that combine to create a mood of robust, if somewhat grumbly, jollity – 'usually ruined', according to Tovey, who knew his Brahms, 'by being played far too fast'. But Brahmsian gruffness, the mood which mars his two cello sonatas and prompted one modern commentator to claim that they 'inspire respect rather than affection', is here largely in abeyance.

One of the most attractive features of Brahms's three piano trios is the way in which the violin so beautifully offsets the cello, creating a blend of tone notably missing from the cello sonatas (wonderful though the second of these works is). The Third Piano Trio, Op. 101 in C minor, sustains the quality, and both works are heard to advantage in the *intégrale* of Brahms's trios by the Florestan Trio, already recommended.

Fifteen

1883
SYMPHONY NO. 3 IN F MAJOR, OP. 90

Allegro con brio   Andante

Poco allegretto   Allegro – Un poco sostenuto

Of Brahms's four symphonies, the Third is the most concise, the most seemingly self-contradictory and the hardest to perform. When unveiled by the Vienna Philharmonic on 2 December 1883, with Hans Richter as conductor, it was hissed by Wagnerians in the audience but praised so extravagantly by the press that Brahms was embarrassed. Brooding about it more than a month later, he reported that its high reputation was undeserved and would merely prompt people to expect more of him than his Fourth Symphony would be able to deliver. That work, when it arrived the following year, was happily no disappointment at all.

Brahms's deliberately unenthusiastic attitude to his own music was nothing new. But the Third Symphony can still be a source of perplexity.

For some conductors – or at least some concert promoters – its quiet ending makes it an awkward work to programme, the assumption being that audiences like an evening to finish with a bang. Its argument, moreover, can seem either sluggish or turbulent, just as its colouring can seem grey or rich in autumn tints, depending on how it is performed. But ambiguity is a feature of many great works, and this symphony is one of them. Why, for instance, was it once nicknamed Brahms's 'Eroica'? There are several answers, none of them obvious.

Even the first movement's big opening chords can seem enigmatic. The first of them stresses the home key of F major. The second carries a topping of F minor. The third, which swings into the main theme, brings back F major but fails to sustain it. By the next bar, the music is again in the minor. For listeners with no ear for tonality, such a description may seem beside the point. Yet, in these chords, the entire symphony is encapsulated, its combination of certainty and uncertainty instantly defined. Only in the finale's quiet F major coda will the argument be wholly resolved. The soft shimmer of string tone, redolent of a certain rival composer's portrayal of magic fire, here contributes a nice piquancy to the symphony's close.

Between first page and last, however, much is tonally at stake. The opening movement is both assertive and sidestepping, unexpectedly escaping at one point from the combined tensions of F major and F minor into the luminous lyricism of a graceful clarinet theme in A major. Yet this, too, is darkened before long by minor-key colouring and, at the start of the central development section, by a passionately sweeping cello version of the clarinet music. Characteristically, Brahms approaches his recapitulation of the movement's symphonic argument by stealth. In the end, the full weight of the opening theme is never quite allowed to ring out. Grandeur dissolves into a peaceful coda, in anticipation of what will happen in the finale.

Meanwhile, the intimate but faintly funereal slow movement is launched by the strains of a wind ensemble which, with brief echoes from the lower strings, maintains a hesitant, slightly uneasy momentum. Clarinet and bassoon contribute sighingly melancholy phrases incorporating a triplet figure which will be heard again in the finale. Only towards the close of the movement do the violins claim their priority with a new melody and a radiantly Brahmsian crescendo.

The tone is darkened again by the aching, arching cello theme which launches the third movement ('please, is no good unless your fingers bleed' was Paul Kletzki's plea to the Scottish National Orchestra while rehearsing this passage), suggesting correctly that this is to be a symphony without a scherzo. With the pulse of a slow, swaying dance, Brahms's *Poco allegretto* forms a minor-key interlude between the major-key meditation of the *andante* and the minor key eruption of the finale, whose violence is in no way diminished by the fact that it starts *sotto voce*.

Coming after what can sound like a pair of spectral entr'actes, the terseness of this movement is all the more unexpected and, with its snarling trombones, all the more ferocious. The music swirls through a succession of abrupt, keenly unified themes, but eventually begins to burn itself out. The pace conspicuously slackens. The flute ascends serenely to a high F. From the storm clouds of F minor, the symphony has reached the safe haven of F major. The first movement's opening chords return, shedding their original ambiguity as the music dies away in tones which are reminiscent of the end of *Die Walküre* but also prophetic of the end of Schoenberg's *Transfigured Night*.

Whatever the problems – of structure, of colouring, of balance, of meaning – encountered in this work, Sir Charles Mackerras's recording with the Scottish Chamber Orchestra solves them in a way which Herbert von Karajan and the Berlin Philharmonic notoriously never did. The SCO's lack of numbers does no damage to a score which requires asperity as well as power, rasp as well as warmth. Mackerras's set of the symphonies has already been recommended in these pages; and here is one more reason for acquiring it.

Sixteen

1885
SYMPHONY NO. 4 IN E MINOR, OP. 98

Allegro non troppo

Allegro giocoso

Andante moderato

Allegro energetico e passionato

Brahms, like Mahler, was a symphonist who sought escape each year from Vienna to the Alpine lakes and mountains which inspired him. The village of Pörtschach on the Wörthersee, where he wrote his radiant Second Symphony in 1877, was one of his favoured spots. Staying in chillier Styria in 1884 and 1885, he reported that 'the cherries don't ever get to be sweet and edible in this part of the world'. As a result, he said, his Fourth Symphony – on which he was at work – was acquiring the flavour of the climate.

It is certainly the most acerbic of his symphonies, less triumphal than No. 1, less idyllic than No. 2, less romantic than No. 3. Tovey called it 'tragic', mainly because it begins and ends in a minor key; but that is not really the right word for it. 'Classical' might be more appropriate, or even 'baroque', on account of its sense of form and of the austerely measured, gravely dancelike nature of all four of its movements.

Not wholly surprisingly, it was once transformed into a ballet entitled *Choreartium*, with choreography by Leonide Massine stressing abstract interplay between male and female movements. This, no doubt, would have shocked Brahms's contemporaries, as well as the composer himself. But it was Eduard Hanslick, the Viennese critic and champion of Brahms, who produced the most striking description of the piece. Hearing it played privately on two pianos prior to its premiere, he said that the first movement made him feel as if he had been thrashed by two tremendously intelligent men.

Vienna was not, in fact, the first city to hear Brahms's last symphony. It was to Meiningen, and its fine orchestra, that that honour went in October 1885, when Brahms himself conducted it, thereafter touring it as far as the Netherlands. The audience was responsive everywhere and, in Meiningen, demanded (but did not receive) a repeat of the scherzo. Yet, although he lived on for a further twelve years after writing it, Brahms produced only one more orchestral work – his somewhat arid Double Concerto for violin and cello – during that time. It would be fair to say, then, that the Fourth Symphony was his culminating orchestral masterpiece.

As a swan-song, it could hardly have been bettered. Its terseness is proclaimed by its opening measures, a series of two-note phrases which rise and fall in such a way that the music seems to start in mid-flight. It was an inspiration innovative enough to distress Brahms's friend and adviser, the violinist Joseph Joachim, who proposed that a short orchestral preamble should be added (as in the 'get ready' rhythm on the violas at the start of Mozart's Symphony No. 40). To this, Brahms sharply replied that he had already written just such a beginning and had deleted it.

The way Brahms builds up the opening theme is the work's first demonstration of mastery. It is followed by a rather baleful fanfare-like tune on horns and woodwind, and by a broad, fiery melody on the cellos. The tension of the music leaves no scope for a conventional repeat of the expository material, such as Brahms had taken pains to incorporate in his three previous symphonies. Instead, he makes a brief pretence of going back to the beginning, then suddenly changes course to startling effect. Even the recapitulation, when it arrives, is far from conventional. The main theme's return, in long, slow notes, is initially veiled and ghostly, yet it is from here that the movement strides off towards its ferociously incisive climax and final hammered-out kettledrum thwacks, by Brahms's standards an unusually theatrical touch.

Nor, at least to start with, does the slow movement provide much balm. The horns blow what sounds like the beginning of a sombre, somewhat funereal march, to which other instruments – clarinets, pizzicato strings – add softer touches of colour. But not until after a passage of violently emphatic triplets does warmth at last arrive in the form of a broad, lush cello melody, which will be heard again later in the movement, played even more richly by divided strings.

The scherzo – and this is the only Brahms symphony to include a genuine scherzo, even though it is in no way humorous and most of it is in hard-driven march-time – is a raw, brilliant, hard-edged tour de force, to which a piercing piccolo and the brittle jangle of a triangle add surface glitter. Towards the end, huge chords from top to bottom of the register suggest that this scherzo might originally have been designed as the symphony's finale; but Brahms had very different ideas about how the work was to end.

Employing the final chorus of Bach's Cantata No. 150 as his model, he composed a substantial set of variations on the eight-note theme which Bach had previously put to the same use. What attracted Brahms to this obscure and, in 1885, still unpublished bit of Bach was the fact that the variations took the form of a passacaglia, a rigorous baroque structure – originally a dance – whereby a given theme is repeated over and over again, usually (though not necessarily) in the bass register.

In Brahms's symphony, Bach's inspirational theme – essentially a rising scale, one note of which Brahms sharpened for the sake of piquancy – is sonorously unveiled by the trombones (whose tonal ballast has been absent from the previous movements) and other wind instruments, plus kettledrums. The theme, surely not by accident, reveals itself to be a sort of upside-down version of the scherzo's main theme – not the only example of this work's remarkable cogency.

The succeeding variations, which are more Brahmsian than Bachian, are unfurled with a powerful, pungent momentum which sometimes stops in its stride to accommodate passages of gentler, slower, more glowing music – the sustained, exquisitely fragile flute variation is probably the best-loved moment in the entire work – before resuming with increased force. Could this, then, be the music of tragedy? Well, perhaps, though only if you want to hear it that way. But it neither needs to sound like that nor, surely, was it ever intended to. It is Brahms at his most gravely and ardently exhilarating, and that is quite enough.

Apart from Sir Charles Mackerras's impeccably direct and sharp-textured performance, based on the size of orchestra which Brahms favoured for the Meiningen premiere (Mackerras's equivalent being the modern-sounding but period-conscious Scottish Chamber Orchestra plus trombones and a few extra strings), the recording of the Fourth Symphony which really rivets attention is Carlos Kleiber's with the Vienna Philharmonic.

The sound-world of this distinguished orchestra is very different from the SCO's, which implies not that it is better or worse but simply that the music is presented in a manner to which more listeners are accustomed. Burnished tone is what we expect from this most famous of orchestras, which was founded when Brahms was nine. Its drawback is that behind the tone lies complacency, and you can see why Brahms liked Hans von Bülow's (subsequently Richard Strauss's) more spirited band.

The galvanising force on this occasion, however, is the brilliant but idiosyncratic Carlos Kleiber, who injects what is essentially a traditional performance with his own flashes of perception. The result, recorded in 1981, remains greatly fresh and alive (DG 457 706-2). It may not oust Otto Klemperer's older, more granitic version of the work with the Philharmonia Orchestra (EMI 5 67031-2), but its grip never slackens.

Seventeen

1891
TRIO IN A MINOR FOR CLARINET, PIANO AND CELLO, OP. 114

Allegro   Adagio

Andante (andantino) grazioso   Allegro

Like Mozart in his Requiem, in *La clemenza di Tito* and in his final concerto, Brahms closed his career to the sound of clarinets. Mozart's muse was his friend and fellow freemason, Anton Stadler, the first clarinettist in the history of music to achieve public fame. Brahms's was Richard Mühlfeld, principal clarinettist in the great Meiningen orchestra and for twelve years at Bayreuth.

Mühlfeld entered Brahms's life, as Stadler did Mozart's, at a time when this single-reed instrument – the 'lordly' clarinet as Mozart called it – provided the sound quality, brightness veiled by melancholy, melancholy illuminated by brightness, which was just what he wanted and needed.

NOTES ON BRAHMS

The peculiar ambiguities of its tone, and its ability to plunge from creamy top notes into the shadows of its bottom register, inspired him to write five works which have become jewels of the repertoire, masterpieces which all clarinettists feel required to master.

Brahms, it has been said, was always an autumnal composer, even if he did most of his composing in summer. The statement, frivolous though it may seem, has enough truth in it to be treated with respect. The clarinet was his autumnal instrument par excellence, which he sometimes allowed to be replaced by the similarly autumnal viola if no clarinettist was available. There are occasions, indeed, when the word seems to be applied too often to Brahms's music, thus diminishing the effect of the works which are truly valedictory.

By the time he reached his Clarinet Trio, Op. 114, however, there was no doubt about the music's implications. He was by then in his late fifties, and sensed that he was soon to die. Even without a clarinet to intensify its message – this was one of the works in which he authorised the viola, another instrument of distinctively Brahmsian timbre, to serve as replacement – the death-consciousness of the music is unmistakable.

Having written his last will and testament in May 1891, Brahms was on the brink of retirement. All around him, close friends were dying prematurely. Back in his native Hamburg, so were members of his own family circle. His musical plans, he said, were confined to the completion of a few unfinished works and – ominously – the destruction of the rest.

It was the strains of his 'dear nightingale', as he called Mühlfeld's clarinet, that kept him going. Summers spent composing in one of his favourite spas or lakeside resorts were in any case a habit he found difficult to break. From 1880 onwards, one of his favourite destinations had been Bad Ischl in the Salzkammergut, and it was there that the A minor Trio was written in the summer of 1891, followed immediately by what he characteristically called 'a far greater folly', his B minor Clarinet Quintet.

The trio, in its original Mühlfeld version, was premiered in Berlin in December 1891, with Brahms himself as pianist. Yet the cello part written for Robert Hausmann of the Joachim Quartet, who had taken part in the first performance of the Double Concerto a few years earlier, was little less important. It is the cellist, indeed, who launches the trio with a high, mournfully singing solo, in the articulation of which the other instruments soon join.

Giving the cello this sort of prominence in such a work would have astonished Haydn and Mozart, whose trios invariably treated the cellist's role as subservient. At times, as one authority has observed, Brahms's trio actually sounds like a cello sonata with a clarinet (or viola) obbligato. The mood of the movement, for the most part, is sombre, and the second subject in E minor, again with a prominent part for the cello, does nothing to lighten it. Not until the coda, with its curious rippling harplike sound effect, does the colour significantly change, though the outcome remains unresolved.

NOTES ON BRAHMS

The austerely beautiful *adagio* brings no great consolation, in spite of its major key and the exquisite interplay of clarinet and piano tone at the start. Though it consists of just fifty-four bars, it is nevertheless the longest, most probing movement of the four. The unhurried waltz which follows, again in the major, is content to be sweet and wistful, hinting at the sound-world of the *Liebeslieder Walzer* but never quite smiling enough to recapture it fully. Often said to be poised somewhere between Schubert and Johann Strauss, the mellowness of the music is in fact wholly Brahmsian. Much of the movement's subtly dancing pulse depends in any case on whether it is performed *andante* or *andantino* (meaning slowly or not quite so slowly), either of these speeds being permissible.

Brahmsian, too, are the changing time signatures which bring a dash of disruptiveness to the rhythms of the minor-key finale. Brahms, like Schubert before him, adored what was regarded in Vienna as the Hungarian style, whose presence here at last brings a vivacious dash of paprika to the flavour of the piece. The result, it's true, does not quite achieve cheerfulness, but gets closer to it than seemed likely earlier in the work.

Recordings of Brahms's Clarinet Trio generally come as part of a package deal, along with his other works in trio form. This is a good, not necessarily too expensive, way to acquire it, especially in the probing performance featuring Philip Hosford with members of the Florestan Trio (Hyperion CDA67251/2). Alternatively, on a single disc, there is

Thea King, whose unhurried phrasing catches the mood of the work to perfection. Joined by the Gabrieli Quartet in the Clarinet Quintet, she is equally persuasive (Hyperion CDA66107).

Eighteen

1891
QUINTET IN B MINOR FOR CLARINET AND STRINGS, OP. 115

Allegro

Andantino – Presto non assai, ma con sentimento

Adagio

Con moto

Towards the end of his life, Brahms was inspired by Richard Mühlfeld, clarinettist of the Duke of Meiningen's court orchestra, to compose a series of works for that instrument in combination with various others – with piano (in the two sweet-sad duo sonatas, Op. 120), with cello and piano (in the poignant A minor Trio, Op. 114) and with a string quartet (in this great B minor Quintet, Op. 115). The composer's characteristic tendency to belittle his own music led him to speak of the trio and quintet as 'twin pieces of foolishness'. In fact, they show him in peak form, the quintet in particular being a masterpiece comparable with the quintet Mozart had written a century earlier for another gifted clarinettist, Anton Stadler.

Wise after the event, we speak today of the elegiac quality of this music, which Brahms composed as his career drifted towards its close. And it is true that the quintet, mellow in tone and melancholy in spirit, provides good reasons for doing so. At the same time, the ease and fluency of the writing, the absence of struggle, are suggestive of increased mastery rather than a faltering hand. Nor does the work lack passion, however much some performers try to subdue it.

Significantly enough, there is a fascinating photograph – reproduced in several books and well worth examining – of a portly but dapper Brahms strolling with an elegant young woman on Vienna's Ringstrasse in 1891, just after he had completed the quintet. The woman was Alice Barbi, an Italian contralto who sang Brahms's songs with the composer as pianist – 'If I were young, I would now write love songs', he declared – and who was much seen in Brahms's company around that time.

But if she did something to rejuvenate the 58-year-old composer, so did Richard Mühlfeld, whom Brahms met in Meiningen and whose exquisite playing instantly held him in thrall. A self-taught clarinettist who had previously been a violinist, Mühlfeld must have possessed – to judge by what Brahms wrote for him – a tone that was subtle and liquid and perhaps (or so it was said) almost feminine in its beauty from top to bottom of the register. Brahms referred to him as 'my Prima Donna'.

The quintet, traditionally described as silver-grey in colouring but by no means devoid of richer tints, opens with a billowing theme, whose liquid rhythm (a dotted crotchet followed by six semiquavers) leaves its stamp on the whole of the first movement. Its melodic contours, moreover, reappear in the main themes of all the succeeding movements, thus helping to give the work a special unity. The clarinet enters at the fifth bar, climbing through a two-octave arpeggio before repeating and expanding the opening theme. A more assertive passage (which will return more musingly later in the movement) leads to another flowing theme, played by clarinet and second violin in unison against a sinewy web of counterpoint. The climax comes towards the end when, with a sudden upsurge, the opening theme rings out strongly before dying regretfully away.

The *adagio* in B major is built principally from a sustained melody sung by the clarinet over a muted accompaniment. This theme is later elaborated in a middle section in the minor, where the music gains a pronounced gypsy flavour and the clarinet articulates passionate arabesques against a darkly tremulous background of strings. It is a passage that thrusts us suddenly and startlingly into the world of Schoenberg's *Verklaerte Nacht*, written eight years later; but the prophetic moment passes, and the movement ends as calmly as it began.

The third movement, a typically Brahmsian intermezzo rather than a scherzo, is a throwback to the equivalent movements of his first two symphonies. First, as in the C minor symphony, the clarinet delivers a smooth, amiable melody. Then, as in the D major symphony, this melody is speeded up in a pattering *presto* section, in which, at one point, the clarinet plays a wistful, syncopated little tune with pizzicato accompaniment, curiously suggestive of Elgar.

Although the third movement and finale are not linked, the one seems to grow naturally out of the other. But the finale – a set of variations veering between vehemence and nostalgia – also has connections with the first movement, as is confirmed by the return of the opening theme at the very end, thereby eloquently bringing the music full circle.

Of Brahms's works for clarinet, this is understandably the most popular and by far the most frequently recorded. Buyers can choose, in particular, between David Shifrin with the Emerson Quartet, Karl Leister with the Leipzig Quartet, Thea King with the Gabrieli Quartet, and Janet Hilton with the Lindsay Quartet, all of them so good that choice of coupling may be what finally governs choice of recording.

Shifrin matches America's leading string quartet in the poise of his playing, and the coupling, Mozart's Clarinet Quintet, is impeccable (DG 459 641-2). Leister and the Leipzigers produce such alertly integrated tone that the clarinettist's absence from the coupling, Brahms's Second String Quartet, may lose this excellent disc some potential buyers (Dabringhaus and Grimm MDG 307 0719-2).

In a class of its own, however, is the historic recording by Reginald Kell and the Busch Quartet, dating from the 1930s and probing every phrase, rhythm, texture and implication of the music like no performers since.

NOTES ON BRAHMS

With the Horn Trio (featuring Kell, Rudolf Serkin and Aubrey Brain) as coupling, this is a performance which remains untarnished by age and has been kept in circulation by two different record companies (Pearl GEM0007 and Testament SBT 1001).

Nineteen

1892
THREE INTERMEZZI FOR PIANO, OP. 117

Andante moderato   Andante non troppo e con molto espressione

Andante con moto

Brahms, like Beethoven before deafness damaged his career as a performer, was an inspired exponent of his own piano music. But, although his youthful panache at the keyboard was what first attracted the attention of Robert and Clara Schumann to him when he dropped in on them in Düsseldorf as a 20-year-old tyro, he devoted substantial portions of his career thereafter to not writing for the piano, except in conjunction with other instruments.

His earliest sonata, inaccurately numbered Opus One, was the work he took to Schumann as a visiting card and so impressed the older composer with his performance of it that Schumann jotted in his diary: 'Visit from Brahms, a genius'. His reference to the not-yet-portly newcomer as 'a young eagle' confirmed his daughter Marie's description of him as 'a very young man, handsome as a picture, with long blond hair'. His arrival on the Schumann doorstep at 11am on 1 October 1853 seemed, at any rate, fateful enough to inspire Schumann to say, characteristically cryptically, that 'this is he that should come'.

Yet Brahms's piano sonatas, compared with Beethoven's or Schubert's, were mere flashes in the pan, as also were the out-and-out virtuoso *Paganini Variations* which followed. Brahms's most meaningful piano music came from the end of his life and took the form of collections of short pieces, so succinct and so personal that they were like paragraphs from a secret diary.

With all his big works behind him, the music is now recognised as a wonderful late crystallisation of all Brahms had learned as a pianist-composer. The succinctness is of a sort you wish he had exploited more often, and the pensiveness – all three of the Op. 117 intermezzi are marked *andante* – brings out an imaginative adventurousness that places the pieces on a par with Chopin's similarly diary-like mazurkas. 'Even one listener is too many', Brahms once said of them; and indeed, so confidential does the music sound that you feel yourself to be eavesdropping on it.

The first intermezzo uses an old Scottish lullaby as inspiration for an apparently idyllic study in tone and harmony. But, as Brahms typically referred to all three pieces as 'cradle songs for my sorrows', the music may not be as idyllic as it seems. The original Scottish folk song speaks of betrayal and abandonment by the child's cruel father, and Brahms's minor-key middle section adds an ominous element to the calm sweetness of the rest of the piece.

The two other intermezzi sustain this sort of harmonic instability. There is always a sense of disquiet behind the otherwise exquisite filigree detail, one of whose subtle characteristics is that melody does not always sit on top of the accompaniment but emerges eloquently from inside the texture.

Though Brahms's sets of short pieces tend to be regarded as interludes in a career devoted to more ambitious things, they hold their own special places in his output. Even the more robust of them, such as the Two Rhapsodies, Op. 79, dating from 1879, just before the massiveness of the Second Piano Concerto, reveal his ability to pare his music down to something infinitely smaller in scale though no less strenuous in style.

These rhapsodies show something of what his power as a pianist must have been like. They are magnificent, leonine concert pieces, very much the obverse of the Op. 117 intermezzi. Why he suddenly wrote them at that fairly advanced moment in his career has always prompted speculation, most of it surrounding Elisabet von Herzogenberg, the former pupil and gifted pianist to whom he dedicated them.

The descriptions *agitato* and *molto appassionato* which he applied to them, along with the restlessness of the music itself, suggest something of Brahms's mood when he wrote them. The fact that he had once confessed to a friend that he was 'afraid of his feelings' for young Elisabet says a bit more. An old pattern, one which had already involved Clara Schumann and would continue to do so, appeared to be repeating itself. And Brahms's old escape route, which was to apply his feelings to music rather than people, was again employed. Elisabet, like Clara, became a muse and adviser, but not necessarily a heartfelt beloved.

In musical terms, which for Brahms were the terms that really mattered, it suited him that way. The B minor surge of the first rhapsody, with its ringing octave passages, says one thing about him. The thoughtful, more stable and ultimately slightly Schubertian middle section in B major, with its gentle references to things already heard, says quite another. Then the passion resumes, stormily sustained until the ambiguous major-key close.

In the second rhapsody, in G minor, there is a different sort of turbulence and a different sort of structure, in this case sonata form. Yet passion is not curbed by classical design. In some respects, the music is even fierier and more relentless, with no soft final answers to turn away wrath.

Wilhelm Kempff always seemed the ideal poetic pianist for Brahms's shorter pieces, particularly the pensive ones. But Radu Lupu rivals him with ease in a disc conveniently containing not only the three Op. 117 intermezzi but also the two heftier Op. 79 rhapsodies, along with other items in wonderfully lyrical, observantly textured performances (Decca 417 599-2). Best of all, if you can afford it, is the American pianist Julius

Katchen's six-disc survey of everything from Op. 1 to Op. 119. Though some of the earlier works are expendable, the first sonata in particular is played with enough conviction to show why Schumann fell for it (Decca 455 247-2).

Twenty

1894
SONATA IN F MINOR FOR CLARINET AND PIANO, OP. 120, NO. 1

Allegro appassionato

Allegretto grazioso

Andante un poco adagio

Vivace

Surrounded by death in 1894 – the conductor Hans von Bülow, the surgeon Theodor Billroth and the Bach scholar Philipp Spitta were friends he lost in quick succession – Brahms at the age of 61 became increasingly aware that his days were numbered. His sister Elise had died in 1892, as had his Viennese pupil and confidante, Elisabet von Herzogenberg. Cholera had claimed Tchaikovsky in 1893 when only 53. But Clara Schumann, his friend for forty years, was still alive – though not, as things turned out, for much longer.

With all this as their background, Brahms's two clarinet sonatas – works which share a single opus number and are the most unified of all his paired compositions — unsurprisingly wear an air of melancholy, shot through with the sort of dancing delicacy whereby the overweight composer added lightness to even his saddest scores. In fact, being subject to mood-swings, Brahms was not wholly unhappy when he composed these works. A photograph taken around that time shows him on his birthday, with the cellist Robert Hausmann standing behind him, caught in the act of 'playing' the plump composer with an imaginary bow, as if he were an enormous cello.

The clarinettist Richard Mühlfeld, also present, was to be the recipient soon afterwards of the two sonatas, which he performed privately at Berchtesgarden with Brahms as pianist. No doubt the subsequent performances at a Clara Schumann reunion in Frankfurt, ahead of the official Viennese premiere, were of the deepest importance to the composer.

Mühlfeld, as we know, did much to revive Brahms's dwindling inspiration in the years immediately before his demise. In 1891, Brahms had vowed to compose no more and had written to his publisher Simrock insisting that anything left behind in manuscript after he died was to be burned. Already a proficient destroyer of his own works, he assured Simrock that he would find little with which to fulfil his request. But he had reckoned without the experience of hearing Mühlfeld play the clarinet. Having done so, he wrote his Clarinet Trio and the great Clarinet Quintet before producing the two clarinet sonatas in which his relationship with the instrument was pared to its essence.

Today, we like to speak of the valedictory quality of these pieces. Indeed, the two sonatas, along with the *Four Serious Songs*, were to be his last major works. All this music is predominantly poignant in tone, the songs dark and wintry, the clarinet sonatas tinted with a touching sweetness. Yet, at the same time, it is hard not to feel that here, right at the end of his career, Brahms was only just beginning to resolve some of the problems that had beset him in his earlier chamber music, especially in terms of clarity of texture. Above all, these works have a very personal pensiveness that brings to mind Brahms's comment about some of his piano pieces of the same period. 'Even one listener', he remarked, 'is too many.'

Mühlfeld, to judge by the music Brahms wrote for him, must have possessed a tone that was subtle and liquid from top to bottom of the instrument's diverse register. His first public performance of the sonatas, with Brahms himself as pianist, took place in Vienna in 1895. The composer was so pleased with the result that he wrote alternative versions of the works for viola, bringing a different, grainier, more shadowy tone quality to the music, but sacrificing some of the clarinet's agile ability to dart with ease from one register to another. Yet agility, except at special moments, is not one of the primary necessities of these works, which, in spite of contrasted tempo markings, tend to move without haste and with a sense of resigned death-consciousness in keeping with Brahms's feelings at the time.

Though marked *Allegro appassionato*, the first movement of the F minor Sonata is a sort of *Valse mélancolique*, a sustained, lyrical flow of melody, much of it subdued yet periodically flaring up with big piano chords in the old Brahmsian manner. The slow movement supplies more of the same, but with a nocturnal stillness even more touching and a musing theme for the clarinet, full of tender twists and turns, which haunts the entire course of the music.

Next comes a characteristic intermezzo of the lightest, gentlest sort, a sad waltz shot through with recollections (or so it would seem) of happier days and, in its middle section, a haunting blend of dark-toned clarinet with shimmering piano notes. Then, in the finale, the composer shakes off his sadness and swings his F minor sonata into F major for a cheerfully pattering rondo which only occasionally sinks into the work's previous mood of Brahmsian regret.

Today, more often than not, the sonatas are separated from each other in performance, but their juxtaposition shows how the one is the direct obverse of the other, the sombreness of the F minor finding its resolution in the warmth of the E flat major. The first movement of the latter, an *allegro* to which Brahms added the word *amabile* (meaning 'amiable' or 'sweet'), suggests as much. It is a seamlessly flowing sonata-form structure in which the clarinet plays a singing role.

But in the scherzo – the last scherzo he was ever to compose – Brahms showed that he could still bite. Though its pace is slower than a marking such as *Allegro molto appassionato* might suggest, the piano's mighty chords, ringing out in the key of E flat minor, give this movement a dark power deliberately at odds with the haunting waltz-theme which is its other special feature. The central trio section, in B major, sounds even more measured, before the scherzo makes its sombre return.

The absence of a true slow movement is compensated for by the finale, a set of variations which moves unhurriedly, as if Brahms were aware that these were the last variations he would write. The music is subdued, a study in gentle colours, rising in intensity only towards the end, when at last, however briefly, it shakes off what Nietzsche once described as Brahms's 'melancholy of impotence'.

Sabine Meyer, most admired of modern clarinettists, performs both works and Berg's Four Pieces for clarinet and piano, Op. 5, in a recording commemorating her appearance at the Spannungen Festival in Germany. Spannungen is not the name of a place but the German word for 'excitements'. Meyer, even in some of Brahms's most reflective music, lives up to it. Herbert von Karajan wanted her to be the first female member of the Berlin Philharmonic – and one can see why.

Here, she is partnered by the young German pianist Lars Vogt, who runs the festival in a converted power station at Heimbach. Though there are fine older recordings by Gervase de Peyer and others, these are performances for today, vividly recorded and greatly alert to the music and all its moods (EMI 5 57524 2).

FURTHER READING

Styra Avins, *Johannes Brahms: Life and Letters* (Oxford, 1997)

Brahms, against expectations, was a good and often amusing letter-writer. As a result, the 800-odd pages of this book are no hardship to read and are filled with witty asides. Strongly recommended.

Leonard Botstein (ed.), *The Compleat Brahms* (Norton, 1999)

Short essays, some better than others, on all the works. Invaluable, and easy to read.

Malcolm MacDonald, *The Master Musicians: Brahms* (Dent, 1990; Schirmer Books, 2002)

The best music-plus-works study of the composer. Larger, finer-detailed, more perceptive and better-written than other books in this useful but uneven series.

NOTES ON BRAHMS

Michael Musgrave (ed.), *The Cambridge Companion to Brahms* (Cambridge, 1999)

Malcolm MacDonald's essay on *Veiled Symphonies* (i.e. the concertos) is one of several fine contributions to a book which makes you think about Brahms afresh.

Michael Musgrave, *A Brahms Reader* (Yale, 2000)

Background reading, mostly, and some of it somewhat nebulous. In the end, however, a real picture emerges.

Charles Rosen, *Critical Entertainments: Music Old and New* (Harvard, 2000)

Mixed bag of musical essays, intelligent and provocative, with Brahms at its heart.

Eric Sams, *The Songs of Brahms* (Yale, 2000)

Though less productive than Schubert, Brahms was a finer song-writer than he has been made out to be. Eric Sams's book, full of insights as well as translations, has been worth waiting for.

Jan Swafford, *Johannes Brahms* (Macmillan, 1997)

Grand-scale modern biography which does not underplay the music.

GLOSSARY

Adagio. Italian term for 'slow', often interpreted as very slow. But can also mean 'comfortable'.

Affettuoso. Italian term for 'with feeling'.

Agitato. Italian term for 'agitated'.

Allegro. Italian term for 'light' or 'fast'. But is an 'allegretto' (meaning, literally, 'a little allegro') slower or faster than allegro? The term is usually accepted as meaning slower, but is irritatingly ambiguous.

Amabile. Italian term for 'lovable', or 'in a loving manner'.

Andante. Italian term for 'at walking pace'.

Andantino. Irritatingly ambiguous Italian term, usually taken to mean a little faster than andante, but which can also be interpreted as a little slower than andante.

Appassionato. Italian term for 'impassioned'.

Aria. Italian term for 'air' or 'song', particularly in an opera.

Arpeggio. Split chord, i.e. a chord whose notes are spread in a harplike manner instead of being sounded simultaneously.

Assai. Italian term for 'very'.

Ballade. Instrumental piece in the style of (or with reference to) a sung ballade.

Baritone. Singer whose voice range lies between that of a tenor and a bass.

Cadenza. Solo passage of varying length, particularly in the first movement of a concerto or in a vocal work, enabling the soloist to display his/her technique in an improvisational manner relevant to the work being performed. Mendelssohn tended to write down his own cadenzas.

Canon. Passage in which a melody performed by one instrument or voice is taken up by another before the previous voice has finished.

Cantabile. Italian term for 'in a singing manner'.

Cantata. A vocal work, often but not necessarily of a religious nature, usually involving solo voices and chorus with orchestra.

Chamber orchestra. Smallish orchestra, usually of up to about forty players, suitable for performing in surroundings more intimate than a large concert hall. Though chamber orchestras have their own established repertoire, symphony orchestras frequently intrude on it, just as chamber orchestras today increasingly invade the symphony orchestra's territory, often with conspicuous, indeed revelatory, success, especially in the case of Mendelssohn's and Brahms's music.

Chromatic. Put simply, a scale which moves in semitones or, in piano terms, one which uses all the black notes as well as the white notes of the keyboard. Chromatic harmony is thus richer than diatonic harmony, which involves only the notes of the normal major or minor scales.

Cimbalom. Hungarian string instrument whose strings are set in a wooden box and struck by hammers, producing mysterious, atmospheric sonorities.

Coda. Italian term for 'tail' or 'tailpiece'. The closing section of a movement, often dramatically expanded by Beethoven, by Mendelssohn in the finale of his 'Scotch' symphony, and by Brahms in the finale of his First Symphony.

Comodo. Italian term for 'leisurely', 'unstrained'.

Con brio. Italian term for 'with spirit'.

Concerto. In Brahms's time, a work for solo instrument (or instruments) and orchestra, involving dramatic contrasts and keener integration than in the works of his predecessors, to the extent that his First Piano Concerto was once described as a work 'with piano obbligato'.

Con moto. Italian term for 'with motion'.

Counterpoint. The combination of two or more melodies or musical figures in such a way that they make musical sense.

Dactylic. Metre based on the repetition of one long beat followed by two shorter ones.

Dominant. The fifth note of the scale. For example, the dominant of the scale of C is the note G, which is four notes above C.

Energico. Italian term for 'with energy'.

Fantasy. A mood piece of some sort, free-ranging and (at least seemingly) improvisational in style. In Bach's day, a fantasy tended to be an elaborate and contrapuntal keyboard piece, often for organ.

Finale. The concluding movement of a work (e.g. symphony, string quartet, sonata) in several movements.

Fortissimo. Italian term for 'very loud'. Abbreviated to *ff* in musical terminology.

Fugue. A type of composition, movement, or section of a movement involving a given number of instruments or voices which enter separately, at different pitches, in imitation of each other.

Giocoso. Italian term for 'in a playful manner'.

Grazioso. Italian term for 'graceful'.

Intégrale. French term for a complete and integrated series of performances of a particular type of work by a single composer, e.g. Beethoven's sonatas or string quartets.

Intermezzo. Interlude. Term much used by Brahms for a short, lightweight, usually calm, sometimes poignant movement in a large-scale work.

Larghetto. Italian term for 'slow and dignified'.

Leggiero. Italian term for 'lightly'.

Maestoso. Italian term for 'majestic'.

Meno mosso. Italian term for 'less quickly'.

Mesto. Italian term for 'mournful'.

Minuet. Dance in triple-time, usually employed by Mozart as the second or third movement of a string quartet, or the third movement of a symphony. The contrasted middle section of a minuet is known as a trio, because there was a tradition for writing it in three-part harmony.

Moderato. Italian term for 'at moderate speed'.

Molto. Italian term for 'very'.

Mosso. Italian term for 'animated'.

Motto, or **motto theme**. A recurring theme, which can have considerable structural importance in the symphonic and chamber music of Mendelssohn's time. Mendelssohn was one of the great pioneers of motto themes, which Wagner employed as 'leitmotifs' in his music dramas.

Non troppo. Italian term for 'not too much'.

Obbligato. Italian term for 'obligatory'. Term applied to an instrumental solo of special importance which stands out from the rest of the orchestra or from a piano accompaniment in, for example, a Schubert song. Some Bach arias, e.g. 'Erbarme Dich' in the *St Matthew Passion*, incorporate obbligato instruments. Schubert's 'Shepherd on the Rock' is accompanied by an obbligato clarinet as well as a piano.

Opera. Music drama or 'sung play', in which the cast sing their roles rather than speak them – though speech is employed in some operas, including, most expressively, Beethoven's *Fidelio*. A vital component of opera is the orchestra, providing far more than a mere accompaniment, with a chorus, large or small, supplying another (though not essential) dramatic dimension. Opera as we know it was born in Italy around 1600, spreading to France, Germany, Austria and other countries, and inspiring many cities to build their own opera houses for its performance. Brahms composed no operas.

Overture. Orchestral prelude to an opera. Beethoven composed four overtures for *Fidelio*, as well as various 'concert' overtures designed for separate performance in a concert hall. Independent concert overtures by Brahms include his *Tragic* overture.

Pianissimo. Italian term for 'very soft'. Pianissimo passages – or entire movements – are a special feature of Mendelssohn's music. Abbreviated to *pp* in musical terminology.

Piano trio. From Haydn's time onwards, a work usually written for piano, violin and cello.

Pizzicato. Plucked note on a string instrument.

Poco. Italian term for 'slightly'.

Prestissimo. Italian term for 'as fast as possible'.

Presto. Italian term for 'fast', often taken to mean as fast as possible (which would in fact be prestissimo).

Quartet. Work for four instruments, or ensemble specialising in the performance of such a work. The art of the string quartet (two violins, viola and cello) was perfected by Haydn, who influenced (and was influenced by) Mozart. The form was developed and expanded by Beethoven, whose sixteen quartets form a major portion of his output, and by Mendelssohn, whose quartets form an important portion of his output.

Romanze. Italian term for 'romance'.

Rondo form. Italian term for what was traditionally the spirited finale of a symphony, string quartet or sonata. The word refers to the fact that the opening theme or section of the movement keeps recurring, or coming 'round' again, thereby forming an essential part of the music's structure. Slow movements can also be in rondo form.

Scherzando. In the manner of a scherzo (see below).

Scherzo. Italian term for 'joke'. Title applied by Beethoven, and to a lesser extent by Haydn, to what until then had been a movement in the form of a minuet. In Beethoven's hands, scherzos replaced minuets in symphonies, string quartets, trios and sonatas. They were generally faster, more volatile and often (though not necessarily) humorous.

Semplice. Italian term for 'simple'.

Sonata. A work for one or two instruments, usually consisting of three or four carefully structured and contrasted movements.

Sonata form. Term describing the structure of what was usually the first movement of a sonata during Mozart's period and later. Put simply, it consisted of an 'exposition', based on two or more contrasted themes, a 'development' section in which the material already heard is altered, developed, broken up or tautened in various ways, a 'recapitulation' in which the introductory material is assembled in something like its original form, and a 'coda' or tailpiece, which rounds the music off or brings it to some sort of closing climax.

Soprano. The highest female voice, ranging from middle C upwards.

Sostenuto. Italian term for 'sustained'.

Staccato. Italian term for 'short and detached', much used by Mendelssohn. Opposite of *legato*, meaning smooth. Signified by a dot over the printed note.

Symphony. Form of orchestral work in several movements, usually of an ambitious nature. Much favoured by Haydn (known as the 'father of the symphony'), Mozart, Beethoven, Schubert, Mendelssohn, Brahms and their successors.

Symphony orchestra. Orchestra designed to perform symphonies and similar works, with enough players to meet the music's demands. Though Haydn and Mozart visualised the use of big orchestras, their works are elucidated more satisfactorily by small ones, now known as chamber orchestras. The development in the size and fire power of the symphony orchestra took place in the nineteenth century, partly through the extra instruments required by Beethoven's Fifth and Ninth symphonies and the music's dramatic demands, and also through the increasing size of concert halls. But size is not everything, and the sound of the 'Eroica' symphony played by a chamber orchestra in a smallish hall can be more startling and enthralling than that of the same work played by a big orchestra in larger surroundings. Brahms's symphonies were written for smaller orchestras than the ones which today, in general, perform them.

Tenor. High male voice, employed by Mozart and Beethoven in operatic and choral works and by Mendelssohn in his oratorios.

Tonic. The keynote of a scale. For example, the keynote of the scale of C is the note C.

Tranquillo. Italian term for 'tranquil'.

Tremolo. Italian term for 'trembling'. The rapid 'trembling' repetition of a single note, or alternation between two notes.

Trill. Musical term for the rapid alternation of the written note and the note above. Trills are traditionally decorative, but in keyboard terms they are a way of sustaining the sound of a note.

Trio. A word with several musical meanings: (1) a work for three instruments, (2) the ensemble which performs such a work, and (3) the name of the middle section of a minuet or scherzo, so called because at one time it was written in three-part harmony. Mendelssohn's and some of Brahms's trios are for piano, violin and cello, a format perfected by Beethoven and generally known as piano trios.

Triplet. A group of three notes of equal duration, written where some other quantity of notes (perhaps just a single note) is implied by the time signature.

Vibrato. Italian term for the rapid vibration in pitch produced by instrumentalists or singers in their performance of a piece of music. Exaggerated vibrato is often described, disparagingly, as 'wobble'. As the history of the symphony orchestra progressed during the twentieth century, so the use of vibrato increased. But, in Brahms's day and before, orchestral vibrato was less of an issue. Performances were vibrato-less, and today many specialist players and orchestras have been learning, with greater and greater success, how to recreate the original sound. Though some listeners regret the loss of a warm bath of vibrato-laden string tone, the compensations in terms of incisiveness and authenticity are manifest. Besides, vibrato-lovers continue to be lavishly catered for by symphony orchestras which perform in the old familiar way.

Vivace. Italian term for 'lively'.